1

Recipe for a Perfect Kenya Holiday

ANIMALS
OF EAST AFRICA

STRIPED HYENA

HODDER AND STOUGHTON

3

Text and pictures © 1960
by C. T. Astley Maberly

Originally published by Howard Timmins
and then by Hodder & Stroughton

First East African paperback edition 1965
This edition 1971
Second impression 1972
Third impression 1975
Fourth impression 1976
Fifth impression 1979
Sixth impression 1981
Seventh impression 1982
Eighth impression 1984

COVER PHOTOGRAPH

THE Publishers gratefully acknowledge
LION CUB *by permission of Mr. Bob Campbell*

Printed in Kenya by Kenya Litho Ltd.,
Changamwe Road, P.O. Box 40775, Nairobi.

ISBN 0 340 15399 7

5

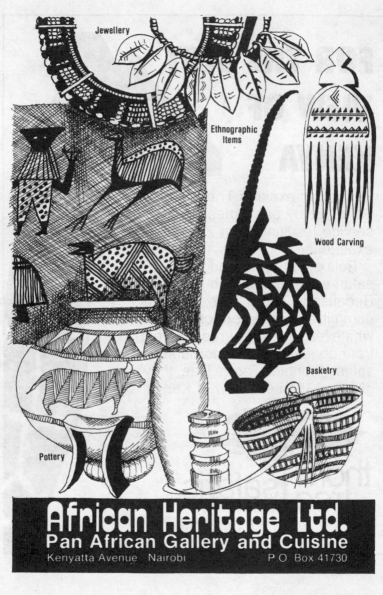

Jewellery

Ethnographic Items

Wood Carving

Basketry

Pottery

INTRODUCTORY NOTE AND
ACKNOWLEDGEMENTS

In order to be able to devote adequate space to the more popularly interesting animals it has been necessary to omit mention of the numerous smaller rodents, bats, etc., which swarm in abundance throughout the areas concerned, and which are equally interesting to the keen naturalist. I have intentionally avoided regular classification order throughout this guide; my principal object being to try to simplify rapid identification in the field by fairly simply defined groups in which—in the case of the numerous species of antelopes—"large," "medium" and "small" are the dominating features: whereas I have simply divided the Carnivora into "large" and "small."

Distribution, in the majority of cases, is entirely confined to distribution in the national parks and national reserves of Kenya.

One or two species of the rarer and more interesting Kenya mammals not at present included in any national park or national reserve have been included for the sake of general interest and information.

The object of the smaller, sketchy "attitude" and "action" sketches included in the illustrations is to indicate typical poses and stances as seen in the field. Most of them are reproduced from my own sketchbooks, and are nature studies from the Parks themselves. Where possible I have included sketches of typical tracks, as these can be of great interest and are often clearly visible in the roads.

To those who are visiting a National Park for the first time, the following suggestions may be of use. First, never drive too fast, because, unless they are right out in the open, wild animals are not easy to spot with the untrained eye. Keep your eyes well focussed in the bush either side of you, and do not concentrate too much on the mere vicinity of the road ahead.

During the hotter hours of the day most animals rest, and they may then very easily be overlooked. Undoubtedly, therefore, the best times to travel in the Parks and reserves are the early mornings and late afternoons, as most things are on the move at those times: and there is always a fair chance of your catching a glimpse of the more strictly nocturnal creatures at such periods. If you are specially keen to see lions, or other of the large *carnivora,* always observe the movements of vultures as these can be of the greatest help. Vultures idly circling round and round high overhead are not of much significance, but if they are gathering from various points and settling in groups on trees or swooping down on to the ground, the neighbourhood is always worth investigating, with good field-glasses if possible. If lions or other large carnivores are busy feeding at a "kill," the vultures will be sitting patiently in the trees, waiting until there is a chance to pounce on the scraps left when the providers of the feast have retired. Without the tell-tale sight of the waiting vultures in the trees, you would probably never suspect the presence of the lions, unless the country was very open and the grass short.

Incessant barking and coughing and congregating of monkeys or baboons may betray a basking leopard, which you would easily pass, even at quite close quarters, so well does he merge with his surroundings! Fluttering white egrets over a swamp may reveal elephant or buffalo lurking there, more or less concealed by the tall vegetation. A concentration of hyenas or jackals also often reveals a "kill" nearby—possibly with lions still there.

Lastly, never get out of your car near lions or elephants or other dangerous game, in order to get a better photograph. However peaceful and harmless they may look when they are not aware of your presence *inside* a motor car, their alarmed reaction at your personal appearance may be startlingly sudden, and in such circumstances the situation could become highly dangerous. The apparent disregard of motor cars by wild animals can be very misleading. You can get so close to them by this means, and they take so little notice, that it is easy to conclude that they are really quite "tame." Make no mistake about it, though! These are completely wild animals, whose very existence depends on their highly developed self-protective instincts. They have learned over the centuries to regard man as the most dangerous of all beings; and even now, in the more friendly atmosphere of National Parks and game reserves, they are still inclined to regard him with suspicion, and his *sudden* appearance at close quarters may easily prompt an impulsive attack in self-defence. In the National Parks and Reserves the wild animals are your hosts in areas especially allotted to them, so treat them with respect and the consideration with which you are wont to treat your human hosts, and you will surely be rewarded with indescribable interest and pleasure. At the same time you will assist in winning their confidence in the presence of human beings!

Among the numerous standard works and publications from which I have quoted reliable information to insure the accuracy of this guide, I must especially acknow-ledge:

The Publications of the *Royal Kenya National Parks.*
Rowland Ward's Records of Big Game (1922 edition).
The Mammals of South West Africa (Shortridge).
The Game Animals of Africa (Lydekker).
Wild Life in South Africa (Stevenson-Hamilton).
A Game Ranger's Note-Book (A. Blayney Percival).
A Game Ranger on Safari (A. Blayney Percival).
Big Game Shooting in Africa (The Londsdale Library).
A Game Warden Among his Charges (Pitman).
Common Antelopes (Pitman).
Game Animals of Eastern Africa (Guggisberg).
The Quarterly publication *African Wild Life,* issued by the Wild Life Protection Society of South Africa.

I am most grateful to Mr. J. L. Fleetwood, Mammalogist of the Coryndon Museum, Nairobi, for so kindly reading through and correcting technical details of my text, and also to Mr. Mervyn Cowie, Director of the Royal National Parks of Kenya, and Mr. Noel Simon, Chairman of the Kenya Wild Life Society, for their assistance and critical suggestions. Finally, I would like especially to thank all those Officials of the National Parks who so kindly and hospitably entertained my wife and me, and gave us such willing assistance during our visit to those areas. Long may the latter survive to guard Kenya's noblest and most precious asset—her incomparable wild animals!

C. T. ASTLEY MABERLY.

LIST OF CONTENTS

THE AFRICAN ELEPHANT

Loxodonta africana (Blumenbach)

(Kiswahili: *Ndovu*, also *Tembo*)

Descriptive Notes.—The African elephant differs considerably from the Asiatic, or Indian, elephant (*Elephas maximus*). It has a more concave, saddle-shaped back: that of the Indian being *convex*, and steeply sloping. The African's enormous, more or less triangular ears, when unextended, cover the shoulders. The small triangular ears of the Indian do not cover the shoulders. The forehead of the African is rounded and sloping: that of the Indian more upright with prominent bulges over the eyes. The formation of the molar teeth is quite different in the two species, and the African has two pointed projections (upper and lower) at the tip of the trunk, whereas the Indian has only one (upper). The tusks are far bigger and more valuable in the African, and normally both sexes grow tusks projecting well beyond the upper jaw (larger and more massive in bulls). Only the male Indian elephant normally grows visible tusks—those of the females rarely project beyond the upper jaw.

Finally, the African elephant is the taller and bulkier of the two species: "an African bull averaging about 10 feet at the shoulder, compared with the ordinary Indian's 9 feet" (Blunt).

Tusks.—The *longest recorded African tusk* measured $11\frac{1}{2}$ feet along the curve. The *heaviest* weighed 235 lbs. The *longest pair* (from East Africa) taped 11 feet $5\frac{1}{2}$ inches and 11 feet respectively, with a *combined weight* of 293 lbs. The tusks of an adult bull (East Africa) may weigh anything from 50-100 lbs. or more. Cow tusks rarely exceed from 15-20 lbs. per tusk. The *record cow tusks* (Uganda) weighed 56 lbs. each.

The record *Indian* tusk weighed 150 lbs.

13

AFRICAN ELEPHANT

"BUSH" ELEPHANT

"FOREST" ELEPHANT

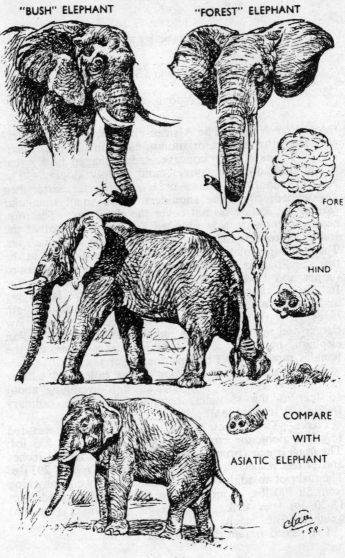

FORE

HIND

COMPARE

WITH

ASIATIC ELEPHANT

Height.—Average height of African bulls measures up to 10 feet 8 or 9 inches at shoulder. Very large bulls of 11 feet or a little over are not uncommon; while bulls up to 12½ feet have been recorded. The average African cow measures about 1½ feet less than a bull.

The *weight* of a bull averages about 6 tons—that of a cow about 4 tons.

Races.—The African elephant has now, generally, been classified into two distinct races.

1. *Loxodonta africana africana*—the "Bush" elephant, which ranges over the scrubs and savannas of East, Central and Southern Africa. Its ear is more triangular, with pronounced lappet; its tusks more massive and curved; and its ivory is "soft"—of greater commercial value as it can be worked more easily. It is the larger of the two.

2. *Loxodonta africana cyclotis*—the "Forest" elephant, confined to the humid, Equatorial forests of West Africa and the Congo. On the average it is smaller in stature (9 feet 7 inches), and has large oval or nearly circular ears with less pronounced lappets. Its tusks are long and slender, usually projecting more downwards from the upper jaw, and its ivory is "hard"—more brittle and less valuable than that of the bush elephant. For those interested in studying ivory and tusk types, a visit to the "Ivory Room" at Mombasa is recommended.

The tail of the African elephant reaches at least to the "hocks," and its tip is fringed with an imposing brush of long, stiff, wiry bristles—sometimes over a foot in length. The bony ridge above the rump is higher in a cow than in a bull.

Distribution.—Plentiful in all the Faunal National Parks of Kenya and in the National Reserves, except in the Nairobi National Park. They have been known to migrate, at certain seasons, within 50 or 60 miles of Nairobi N.P., but none had been recorded since 1942 until two elephants wandered within a few miles of the Park in 1955. They appear up to 12,000 feet in the Mount Kenya N.P., and have been recorded at 16,000 feet on Kilimanjaro. Big tuskers, carrying anything over 100 lbs. of ivory, are not uncommon at Marsabit; and the eastern section of Tsavo National Park (and within 50 miles to north and east of it) has always been renowned for big tuskers.

Habits.—Elephants are gregarious, associating in herds up to several hundreds—though more commonly the average herd probably numbers from about ten to twenty head. Such herds usually consist of a mature bull (a "large beast with tusks of 35-40 lbs. or more"—B. D. Nicholson), one or two younger bulls, and cows and calves. At certain seasons, and for migrating in severe drought, several large herds may amalgamate, thereby aggregating several hundreds—forming a truly wondrous spectacle. Older bulls usually dwell either singly or in pairs or in small groups, leading an exclusively masculine existence, though they temporarily rejoin the main herds for breeding purposes. They probably dislike the constant noisiness of the main herds of cows and calves and young bulls. Elephants can be very noisy. A drinking herd produces a variety of sounds: ranging from abrupt, squeaky notes made through the trunk, and a prolonged, deep vibrating rumble—to short, nasty screams of anger made by quarrelling youngsters, or perhaps by an angry cow admonishing an unruly calf. When charging an enemy a succession of nerve-racking, loud, trumpeting screams may be uttered.

In a calf, the upper edge of the ear remains upright when the ear is cocked. With increasing age it tends to lop over backwards.

Elephants feed mainly on leaves, tender shoots, bamboo shoots in the higher mountain forests, the pithy flesh surrounding palm nuts, reeds and papyrus bordering rivers or swamps, seed pods, and wild fruits, roots and bark. Grass is twitched up by the trunk. Even large trees are broken or pushed over to get at roots or foliage: sometimes several individuals combining to push over a really big one. The base of the trunk or forehead is used—sometimes with the assistance of a foreleg—during such manoeuvres. The tusks are used for levering, or for digging out roots.

In the drier areas, elephants perform a vital service for all other animals by locating water in sandy river beds and digging small wells. "They take up positions at depressions, scuffle out the sand, and then stand quite rigid and silent until the water percolates through" (Mervyn Cowie).

16

Their efficiency at finding the easiest gradients over rugged, hilly or mountainous country led many of the pioneer roads to be constructed over ancient, well-used elephant paths.

Breeding.—Puberty is reached in 10-12 years, and breeding has been known to begin at 13, though usually later. Prime of life is probably reached between 40 and 50 years. It is known that elephants are very long-lived, but exactly how much longer than man's is their potential longevity is not yet known for a certainty. *Gestation period* is stated to be about eighteen months for a female calf, and about twenty-two months for a male calf. Weaning lasts for two years. The two nipples of the cow are situated between her forelegs, and the baby calf suckles with its mouth—its tiny trunk bent back over its head. A cow may be accompanied by three calves of different ages.

Although it is commonly stated that the male Indian elephant comes in season, and not the female, and that during such periods *("Musth")* his condition is made evident by an oily discharge which visibly oozes from the temporal glands (roughly between eye and ear), it appears that the African elephant is different in this respect, for the female, not the male, comes in season—according to well-informed observers. The above-mentioned oily discharge occurs periodically in both male and female, and even in baby elephants, and appears to have no direct sexual significance. Sheldrick has witnessed mating on three occasions, and "neither sex appeared to be in 'musth' at the time." African elephants in the wild state do not appear to be more aggressive or dangerous when showing this discharge, as is apparently the case with the Indian species.

Unmolested, African bull elephants are generally more placid than the more nervous and irritable females; and the latter with small calves are apt to be dangerous at close quarters and should be given a wide berth. Elephants, generally, are temperamental and rather unpredictable in mood, and should always be granted right of way when encountered close to a road.

The average walking pace is estimated at 4 miles per hour. This can be increased to 10 m.p.h. (in a long shuffling stride) under alarm. Its great length of stride enables an elephant to cover ground very quickly, even at

17

a slow walk. Lyell states that a charging elephant, or a very frightened one, can easily attain a speed of 20-25 miles per hour, but only for a limited distance.

Elephants usually drink at night, or in the very late afternoon. From the cottages of the Aruba Safari Lodge in the Tsavo Park they may often be watched drinking at the Aruba dam. So powerful a beast as the adult elephant has no natural enemy, after man; but there are records of young elephants attacked and killed by lions. This has been mostly, of course, when the former have been either orphaned, temporarily separated from the mother for some reason, or else seriously injured. There have been several instances recorded where elephants have attacked and killed crocodiles—especially when the latter have been encountered travelling overland between one pool or river and another.

The trail of elephants is frequently littered with fallen trees or branches, broken off and "barked" twigs, bits of bark and scattered foliage: and of course the great, more or less circular droppings of fibrous and woody matter. In dust, or sand, the huge roundly oval tracks are clearly visible, with the wavy, rugged skin of the sole clearly imprinted upon them.

THE BLACK RHINOCEROS

Diceros bicornis bicornis (Linnaeus)

(Kiswahili: *Kifaru*)

Descriptive Notes.—Shoulder height from 5 feet 6 inches to 5 feet 9 inches in bulls. Females up to 4 feet 10 inches. *Weight* about two tons. *Length,* about 11 feet from tip of snout to base of tail. *Circumference round belly* about 10 feet.

The two horns (not really horn at all, but composed of *closely-packed hair-like fibre growing from the skin,* resting in a slightly hollowed base on the skull, from which they can be detached) are normally present in both sexes. The front horn rises above the nostrils, the rear one almost over the eyes. Occasionally the rear horn is as long as, or even longer than, the front horn.

Front horns have measured up to 43 inches, rear horns up to 21 inches. The majority of front horns in East Africa are probably under twenty inches, but the horns are said to grow longer in the forest-haunting rhino than in those of the dry, thorny plains. The celebrated "Gladys" and "Gertie" (believed to be mother and daughter) of Amboseli had exceptionally long and projecting front horns, and that of Gertie was estimated as possibly reaching four feet.

Upper lip rather pointed and prehensile, as the beast is a browser. Feet relatively small and compact, having three toes on each foot: the central one broad and the lateral ones smaller—producing a characteristic track like the Ace of Clubs! Tail moderately long and scantily tufted at tip.

*Distribution.—*Uncommon and rarely seen in Nairobi National Park; though 5 are at present recorded in the thicker forested area, whence they only emerge at night, and so are occasionally seen only by lucky visitors in the very

19

BULL

COW WITH EXCEPTIONAL
HORNS

early mornings. Rhino appear up to 11,000 feet in the Mount Kenya N.P. and can be seen at "Treetops." They are plentiful in both east and west sections of the Tsavo N.P.; in Marsabit, N.R.; and in Mara, N.R. The real "Show-place" for Rhino in Kenya, however, is the Ol Tukai area of Amboseli National Reserve. Here, as many as seventeen of these beasts have been seen by fortunate visitors "before breakfast," and remarkably fine views of them can be obtained in the vast stretches of open, dusty country, varied with groves of beautiful yellow-stemmed Acacia forest, with a background dominated by glorious snow-capped Kilimanjaro.

Habits.—The black rhinoceros is essentially a browser off thorny twigs and shoots, though it may occasionally eat certain grasses. For this reason its upper lip projects, and is somewhat prehensile, to enable it to grasp foliage. It is found in a greater variety of country, and has always had a wider distribution in Africa, than its larger square-mouthed cousin—the White rhinoceros. In colour both species actually are similar—a dull grey, though as they both like to roll and wallow in muddy pools or swamps, their hides take on the colour of the local soil.

The black rhino feeds mainly by night and in the early mornings and late afternoons, spending the heat of the day resting in the shade, often lying down on haunches or flanks like an enormous pig. It is always accompanied by its faithful guardians—the "Tick" birds (*Buphagus*) which incessantly cling to, or clamber about, its huge frame, eagerly extracting the ticks with which the rhino are burdened. At the first cause of alarm, these birds fly up with chirring cries, and the slumbering, dozing, or feeding rhino is instantly on the alert. Its eyesight is exceedingly poor (it probably cannot distinguish a motionless object beyond fifteen yards), but hearing, and especially scent, are good. When suspicious, it will stand perfectly still, ears cocked and grotesque head raised, nostrils widely dilated as it searches the wind. If its fears are confirmed, it will either utter a few penetratingly loud, blast-like snorts, loop its tail over its rump, and trot away at a slinging, rather zigzag, pace through the scrub until it finally wheels round to stare and snort once more; or it may elect to lower its massive head and come at a lumbering

21

gallop straight for the cause of its alarm: such "charges" in the majority of cases being merely impulsive and confused rather than deliberately aggressive. Provided there is time, they can usually be dodged! Nevertheless, although they are becoming used to traffic at Amboseli and the more popular areas of Tsavo, the Director of National Parks cautions that rhino should never be trusted, and should be given a reasonably wide berth.

The black rhino is an odd mixture of inquisitiveness, stupidity and nervous irritability; and there is little doubt that its poor eyesight contributes to the latter (although the equally "blind" white rhino is lethargic and placid). It has been known to charge an oncoming train, twice in succession—in each case coming off second best at the encounter: and a cow rhino, accompanied by her calf, twice charged the carcase of a dead elephant which lay in her path, before finally ambling disgruntedly away!

The rhinos at Amboseli were remarkably good-tempered and tolerant when we visited them, even though the warden permitted us some very close views from his jeep. It is generally agreed that black rhino often differ temperamentally in different areas—this no doubt being due to the degree of relative peace or persecution they suffer in their neighbourhood. Thus, in the northern area of the Tsavo Park the rhino are very aggressive owing to constant persecution from native poachers until recently. For this reason, that area of the Park is at present closed to the public. An example of a really "bad" rhino comes from Ngong National Reserve, where, in 1955, a bad-tempered bull rhino had to be shot after he had caught four Masai in succession. His custom was to wait near a cattle track leading through broken country to the Ole Debesse wells, and to charge any cattle or herdsman that passed that way.

Rhino usually drink at night, sometimes travelling long distances to water. They are noisy, and very quarrelsome, when they sometimes gather at a solitary waterhole: chasing one another about and scrapping over "water rights." On such occasions they produce some extraordinary noises—ranging from deep, hippo-like grunts or short roars to high-pitched squeals of indignation, and of course the usual snorts.

The usual gait is a fairly fast walk, head lower than

shoulders but held almost horizontally. This is varied with a shambling, rather bouncing trot: and in extreme alarm, or when charging, it is increased to a gallop: in the latter case the head is lowered with the front horn projecting horizontally. In attack, an attempt is made to "toss" the victim with the front horn. When alarmed, a rhino runs away with its tail cocked or looped over its rump.

The female always walks or trots ahead of her calf.

Breeding.—Rhino are slow breeders. Three years are said to elapse between the birth of each calf, and the period of gestation is from 11 to 13 months. Gertie, of Amboseli, produced a calf (known as "Pixie") born with the abnormality of having no external ears.

When standing or feeding in the thick, scrubby stuff often growing round anthills, or in other thickets, rhino are exceedingly hard to spot, and they may easily be passed at quite close quarters by visitors who do not maintain an observant watch.

The Rhinoceros is very greatly persecuted by native poachers for the sake of its horns, which, in powdered form, are in great demand in certain oriental countries for believed "Aphrodisiac" properties. Unscrupulous traders at the coast will obtain extremely high prices for this commodity, consequently the poaching "racket" is a severe one in Africa: and the use of the poisoned arrow a deadly threat to the continued survival of the Rhinoceros except in the most carefully guarded National Parks and National Reserves.

A curious habit of the Black Rhinoceros is that of repairing regularly to selected places in which to deposit its dung: heaps of which accumulate at such points. After voiding, the dung is often kicked and scattered about with the hind feet, and sometimes rootled about with the front horn.

THE ZEBRA'S

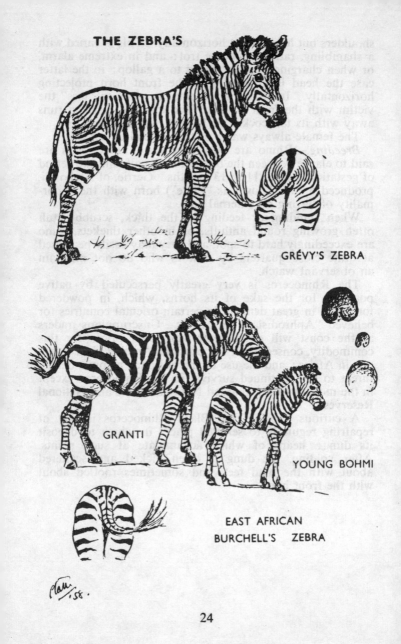

GRÉVY'S ZEBRA

GRANTI

YOUNG BOHMI

EAST AFRICAN
BURCHELL'S ZEBRA

THE ZEBRAS

1. EAST AFRICAN BURCHELL'S ZEBRA

Equus burchelli granti (Lydekker)
Equus burchelli boehmi (Matschie)

(Kiswahili: *Punda milia*)

Field Impression.—Pony-like in build: stripes on rump *broad*: ears short and narrow.

Descriptive Notes.—Burchell's species of Zebra is the most widely distributed one in Africa; ranging, in several locally differing subspecies, from northern Kenya to Zululand. The extinct Quagga of the plains of the Cape and Orange Free State, in which the ground colour was rufous-bay, with stripes only on head, neck, and forepart, is now believed to have been the most southerly race.

The Northern East African subspecies is almost pure black and white *(Granti);* but in southern Kenya and in Tanganyika feint, but definite intervening "shadow" bands sometimes occur between the pure black and white striping on the haunches *(Boehmi).* The more southerly races, south of the Zambesi, have very definite dusky shadow bands imposing on the decidedly more creamy ground between the dark stripes (here dark brown rather than black): sometimes extending along the barrel; and the stripes below knees and hocks are broken, irregular, and sometimes non-existent.

Zebras vary a great deal in one herd, and in the Nairobi National Park you can see individuals with no shadow bands at all, and others with more or less evident indications of them. The striping is continued regularly down the legs to the hooves in the East African Burchell's Zebra, and the ground colour is whiter, and the stripes richer and blacker than in southern types.

What is very noticeable about the East African *Burchelli*

25

is the shorter mane, with hardly any forelock, in the adult. The southern subspecies have more upstanding manes with pronounced, forward-curved forelocks—such as are present in *immature* animals of the East African type.

The barrel stripes meet under the body in the forepart; and the very broad black stripes along the rump run downwards from the horizontal towards the belly. Sexes are alike. In foals the coat is rougher, and the stripes browner, than in adults.

Height of a stallion: up to 4 feet $3\frac{1}{2}$ inches (12 hands).

Weight from 500-700 lbs.: mares are usually heavier and bulkier than stallions, according to Selous.

Length. about 8 feet (from nose to base of tail).

Tail: the brush of black and white hairs at tip reaches as far as the hocks, sometimes just below.

Distribution.—Nairobi National Park; Amboseli National Reserve; Tsavo N.P.; Mara N.R., and Marsabit, N.R. Zebra are not found in the mountain National Parks. Where present, they are always plentiful, occurring widely in most East African game areas in suitable country.

Habits.—Burchell's Zebra are gregarious, associating in herds ranging from half a dozen or so to fifteen or twenty; sometimes congregating in many hundreds (even thousands) of individuals when on migration during the dry season. Their richly striped forms, and the fact that they are the "wild horses" of Africa, lend them spectacular interest. They frequently associate with Wildebeest, Kongoni, Topi, and Ostriches on the open plains. The shorter heads and shorter ears of Burchell's Zebra give them a more horse-like build than the longer headed and larger eared Grévy's and Cape Mountain Zebras.

They are noisy, restless creatures; and when alarmed, or assembling at drinking places (or when otherwise excited) constantly utter a very characteristic, *barking* whinny. This is frequently repeated, and sounds like: *"Kwa ha! Kwa-ha! Kwa-ha-ha-ha!"* Zebras are purely grazing animals, occurring most plentifully on open, grassy plains or in well-grassed, lightly wooded savanna or thorn bush, at various levels. They are very dependent on water, and are subject to great regular annual migrations, in search of grazing and water, at the end of the dry season. Zebra are favourite prey of lion, but are more wary and alert than wildebeest. They are usually infested with grass ticks. In defence, both hooves and teeth are used; and a good deal of biting and kicking goes on at a water-hole.

"Burchell's Zebra frequently lives to over 12 years, and has been known to reach an age of between 28 and 29 years" (Flower).

Foals are usually born in East Africa in February—March.

The Spoor is larger than that of a donkey but narrower than that of a horse.

2. GREVY'S ZEBRA

Equus (dolichohippus) grevyi (Oust)

(Somali: *Fer'o;* Ndorobo: *Kanka*)

Field Impression.—Tall and mule-like; stripes *exceedingly narrow* and close-set; belly white; unmarked; ears large and broad.

Descriptive Notes.—Grevy's is the tallest and most beautiful of the Zebras. It stands as much as 14 hands at the shoulder, and is very characteristically marked with closely set, very narrow black or dark brown stripes on a white or creamy ground (the Somaliland individuals are said to be duller in tone than those of Abyssinia and Kenya). The black and white stripes on body, head and limbs are very narrow, widening out only on the lower jaw, neck and lower part of thigh. There is a broad dorsal stripe, wider near middle of back, and the upper part of the rump is marked with vertical stripes arranged concentrically round the root of the tail. *Underparts clear white,* without transverse stripes. Stripes on the nose stop short of nostril patches—the nose itself being greyish (Lydekker). Mane thick and high, extending on to withers. *Ears large* broadly tubular and heavily fringed. Legs striped narrowly right down to hooves.

27

Distribution.—Only from northern Kenya, from the Tana river, to eastern shores of Lake Turkana; thence to Abyssinia and eastwards to Somalia. Grévy's Zebra occur only in the *Marsabit National Reserve,* and in no other present Kenya National Park or National Reserve. In the Marsabit area they are plentiful. Grévy's is the most northerly representative of the Zebras.

Habits.—Grévy's Zebra inhabits open or not very thickly wooded country of the thorny "scrub" type. It is frequently found on barren, arid plains, even stoney country. It is frequently associated with Beisa oryx. The lion is its principal natural enemy. In 1906, the late Blayney Percival, first Game Warden of Kenya, shot an albino Grévy's Zebra mare on the plains near the Lorian Swamp, and this is mounted in the British Museum (Natural History). He described her as "pure white with the faintest of cream stripes; the eye white, like those of a wall-eyed horse."

The cry of Grévy's Zebra is quite different from the barking call of Burchell's Zebra. It *brays* more like a donkey, the sound being described as a "very hoarse kind of grunt, varied by something approaching a whistle; the grunts being long-drawn out and divided by the shrill whistling sound, as if the latter were made by drawing in the breath which had been expelled during the sustained grunt" (Neumann). Incidentally, such a long-drawn whistling sound sometimes precedes the barking call of Burchell's.

Grévy's Zebra run in small herds of half-a-dozen to thirty individuals. The foals are usually born in August or September. The spoor of Grévy's Zebra is distinctly larger, and rounder, and more horse-like than that of Burchell's Zebra.

28

AFRICAN BUFFALO

Syncerus caffer caffer (Sparrman)

(Kiswahili: *Mbogo*, sometimes *Nyati*)

Field Impression.—Large, massive, cattle-like; black; with enormous downward-spreading, widely curved horns; ears broad and drooping.

Descriptive Notes.—Very bulky and massive in build, with comparatively short muzzle. Dull black, but in old bulls the hair becomes very scanty, resulting in a greyish tone. Calves and younger animals have a decidedly browner tinge. Bulls stand about 5 feet at shoulder, cows about 4 feet 10 inches. A large bull weighs up to 2,000 lbs. Hair of coat rather coarse, and the tail is only moderately long, cattle-like with a scanty fringe or brush at its tip. Ears broad and downward drooping, fringed tips.

Horns.—Good bulls carry anything from 30-40 inches along outer curve. The $56\frac{1}{4}$ inch record head, from Kenya, measured 44 inches between the horn tips; and the width of the palm, measured on the face of the horn, was $10\frac{1}{4}$ inches. In adult bulls the horns broaden out over the forehead into an almost converging mass, at the top of the head. In cows, the horns are more slender and shorter, with less "boss," more backwardly directed. In young animals the horns at first grow upwards and slightly backwards, and in very old bulls the tips become almost entirely worn away.

Distribution.—Rare in Nairobi National Park, which it visits from time to time from the neighbouring Ngong Hills Reserve where a few remain. Tsavo National Park; Amboseli National Reserve; Mount Kenya National Park and in the Aberdare Forest N.P. They are plentiful in Marsabit National Reserve.

Habits.—Buffalo are among the most formidable of African big game, and their only natural enemy is the lion,

29

BULL ♂

COW ♀

Clair
58.

30

which prefers to pick out a calf, or cow, when possible. Old solitary bulls are often killed by lions, frequently after prolonged battle during a concerted attack; though lions are not uncommonly fatally injured or killed in such a struggle. Intelligent and cunning, often schemingly vindictive, in attack, the African Buffalo ranks among the most dangerous of game when wounded; and once it charges its opponent (which it does with head well up, only lowering it to toss at the last moment) it can rarely be halted or turned by anything less than a fatal bullet. Unmolested, however, the Buffalo is normally peacefully disposed, placid and rather shy. Buffaloes wandering about in national parks or reserves, or lying or standing lazily chewing the cud, appear as harmless as cattle. Except when a cow has a young calf with her, or in the case of a solitary, bad-tempered old bull, they are no more dangerous than other game in such circumstances.

At Ruindi, in the Parc National Albert of the Congo, the writer had old buffalo bulls contentedly grazing within 50 yards of him, as he sat on an anthill sketching them! It was amusing to note white-necked ravens frequently perching on their massive backs—completely disregarded.

Buffalo are grazers and are never found very far from water of some sort. They prefer lush river valleys with good, sweet grass; open, grassy plains; and the vast beds of reeds or papyrus bordering rivers or swamps, and mountain forests where there are forest glades or surrounding pasture. They are gregarious, running in herds up to a hundred or more; though old bulls are often found solitary, or in pairs (common), or in groups of four or five. Sight, hearing and scent are all good, but with age hearing and sight become poor. The calving period in East Africa is said to be principally between December and February (though we found a dead, prematurely born calf near the Tsavo river in early October.)

Buffalo enjoy wallowing in muddy pools. They are often accompanied by Tick Birds or Cattle Egrets, and the white forms of the latter, fluttering about reedbeds or papyrus swamps, often betray the presence of buffalo (or elephant) concealed within.

The walking gait is slow and ponderous: massive head

31

PATTERSON'S ELAND   (LARGE)

BULL

♂

♀

COW

clau '58

carried below shoulders, muzzle somewhat upthrust: tail occasionally languidly switched from side to side. When stampeding, buffalo crash through the bush in a formidable mass, uttering loud snorts of alarm, and raising clouds of dust in dry country. A charging bull utters coughing grunts of rage, and a wounded one is said to bellow when about to die. Calves "moo" like domestic ones. When a herd is threatened by lions, it forms a defensive semi-circle, with the bulls on the outer flank, and the cows and small calves in the centre. I once watched four buffalo bulls charge, and drive off, a stalking lion in the moonlight.

The spoor, and droppings, of buffalo, are almost identical in size and form with those of cattle.

LARGE ANTELOPES

PATTERSON'S ELAND

Taurotragus oryx pattersonianus (Lydekker)

(Kiswahili: *Pofu*)

Field Impression.—Very large, cattle-like build, with horns straight back and spiralled at base (in both sexes). Rufous-fawn with several vertical white stripes. Old bulls greyer. Tail tufted.

Descriptive Notes.—The largest, and heaviest, of the antelopes. An adult bull stands from 5 feet 7 inches to 6 feet at top of its humped shoulder. *Length* about 11 feet from nose to root of tail. Cows stand rather less in height. *Weight* of a bull from 1,500 lbs. to 2,000 lbs.

The East African Eland is a rather rich-coloured (more bay or rufous-fawn tinted) animal than the South African type, with more pronounced white stripes down its flanks. There is a conspicuous black band across the hinder part of the foreleg, above the knee. A long dark line marks the top of the back, assuming the form of a slight, ridged mane along the humped shoulder. There is a prominent dewlap below the neck from which projects a tuft of dark hair near the chest. Middle line of face, above and below the eyes, dark brown to blackish: sides of forehead rufous. There is often an indistinct white chevron between the eyes. Old bulls have a dense "bush" of matted hair, often strong-smelling, on the forehead, and enormously thick and massive necks. Owing to the scantiness of their coats, such old bulls look smoke-grey—more rufous along the hindquarters. *Tail* long, with dark tuft at tip.

Horns.—Present in both sexes, extending straight back and slightly upwards from the head: ruggedly twisted and spiralled at base, smooth and pointed at tips. Bulls horns are very massive and stout: cow horns usually longer but narrower. Male horns average about 27 or 28 inches (Record, 32¼ inches). The Record cow horns measured 43½ inches. Horns of cow Elands are often curiously malformed.

Distribution.—Nairobi National Park; Marsabit National Reserve; Tsavo N.P. (East); Mara, N.R.; The Aberdares and Mount Kenya. It has been recorded at 16,000 feet on Kilimanjaro. This East African subspecies was named after the late Colonel Patterson (of *Man-eaters of Tsavo* fame) who shot the "type" near the Angarua river in 1906. Captain A. T. A. Ritchie has suggested that possibly the finest Kenya eland are found in the Voi-Taveta area, and in the Nairobi area.

Habits.—The huge size and humped shoulders, and the massive necks of the bulls, render eland easy to identify even at a distance. Eland are principally browsers on various leaves and young shoots, pods, wild fruits, etc., though they also eat young grass. They are great travellers, and at certain seasons the usually small herds of from five to twenty-five or thirty animals, combine in larger herds (sometimes up to a hundred or more) for migration. This, oddly enough, is stated to take place mainly during the rains, and is not connected with water supply—as is the case with most of the migratory *grazing* antelopes.

Heavy and bulky as they are, Eland can be surprisingly active, and Captain Pitman records a case where an 8-foot enclosure was easily vaulted by a large, heavy bull. Their normal pace is a walk, increased to a rapid trot under mild alarm. When really frightened they gallop but usually only for a short distance. On such occasions individuals sometimes vault over another's back. A herd of 33 Eland which I watched in Ngorongoro Crater, Tanganyika, consisted of cows, younger beasts and calves, some of which were quite small (June 17th). Only one really big bull accompanied this herd. The long narrow horns of the cows varied enormously, some pointing straight back, others pointed outward at tips, while a few had the horns curved back and almost downwards at the tips. Another smaller herd contained two bulls—one younger than the other. Although the big fellow was amorously disposed towards some of the cows, he displayed no jealousy towards the younger bull. These Eland occasionally uttered a sort of belching grunt.

The lion is the principal natural enemy of the adult Eland, though wild dogs may occasionally attack them. In spite of their size, Eland are remarkably gentle and inoffensive, and I do not think that even a wounded one has been known to charge. It seems a pity that there has apparently been little effort to domesticate so potentially valuable an addition to our domestic stock.

The spoor of the Eland is somewhat elongated and about as large as that of buffalo, but is neater and more compact. Eland suffer very badly from rinderpest, and they were nearly wiped out in East Africa during the bad epidemic which, introduced by Somali cattle, swept down Africa at the end of the last century.

BONGO

Boocercus eurycerus isaaci (Thomas)

Field Impression.—A large, robust, Eland-like antelope, but with no dewlap. Horns twisted in a spiral like those of a giant bushbuck, brilliant rufous to chocolate brown, richly striped with white. Sharp white crescent on chest and white markings on face.

Descriptive Notes.—Height about 48 inches at shoulder. The colour varies from bright chestnut to dark brown.

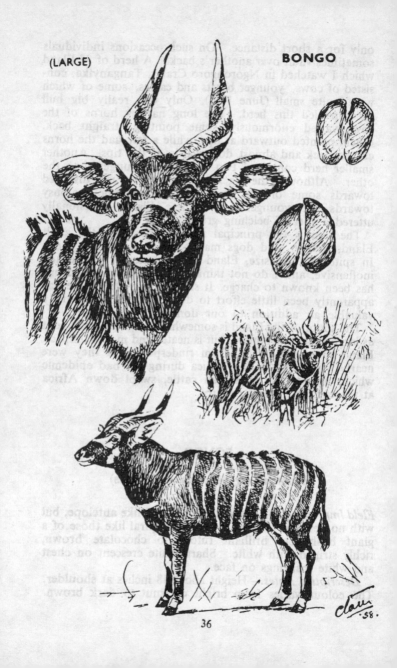

Head, neck and chest from chocolate to almost black. A broad white chevron between the eyes, and two large white spots on cheeks. A sharp crescent adorns the lower part of the throat, just above the chest; and about thirteen barrow white vertical stripes mark the body and rump—being continued up over the erectile dorsal ridge of longer hairs. Legs black, with white patches on the inner surface. Tail tufted, like that of an eland. Ears broad, fringed with white hair. Sexes alike, but old bulls become dark-brown to almost black.

Horns.—Present in both sexes, those of the females longer but narrower than those of males. They have a smooth, open spiral, and are like the horns of bushbuck on a giant scale. The tips wear ivory. Horns average 22-33 inches, the record for the Kenya race being $39\frac{1}{2}$ inches (a female).

Distribution.—In Kenya, Bongo are confined to the high forests, where they are rarely seen unless carefully hunted for. They are numerous in the Aberdare-Kinangop range, and parts of the Mau forest. They also occur in the lower forest of the Chepalungu.

Habits.—The Bongo is the most brilliantly marked of the African antelopes, and it is unfortunate that it is so difficult to see in its secluded forest home. The Kenya form is said to be brighter rufous than the typical West African race. In the Aberdares, according to Major H. C. Maydon, Bongo particularly relish a stingless type of nettle which flourishes in patches among the undergrowth. He also came to the conclusion that Bongo depend more on their ears than on sight or scent, especially as wind in the forest is so elusive. He stresses the difference in colour between big bulls and cows; the bulls being very dark brown to black (rather mangy) in body colour, whereas the cows are light red-brown. The markings on the legs, and the band across base of neck are grey, instead of white as in a cow.

Bongo are generally found in small family parties, but the big bulls are often solitary. They are fond of the pith and rotten wood from fallen trees, and are said to uproot small trees, digging underneath and levering with the horns, in order to get at the roots which they eat.

The spoor is like that of an eland in size and shape.

ROAN ANTELOPE

(LARGE)

♂
BULL

♀
COW

YOUNG

Clam
'58

38

Bongo do not bark, like most of the Tragelaphine antelopes, but are said to utter a grunt, like Eland. They charge angrily when wounded.

EAST AFRICAN ROAN ANTELOPE

Hippotragus equinus langheldi (Matschie)

(Kiswahili : *Korongo*)

Field Impression.—Large, rufous-grey, wiry coated; with short mane on back of neck. Long, tufted-tipped ears, *black and white face* markings; and short, stout, backward-curved ridged horns (both sexes).

Descriptive Notes.—Roan come next to Eland in stature, though more lightly built. A bull stands up to 15 hands high at shoulder (between 50 and 57 in.). Weight between 500 and 600 lbs.

The most conspicuous feature is the black and white face (the forehead is browner in cows and young), with conspicuous white tufts in front of the eyes, and white round muzzle. Next in importance are the long, narrow (almost donkey-like) ears, tufted at their extremities. The coat of the neck and body is coarse and wiry, grizzled rufous-fawn, or greyish-fawn, darker above and paling almost to white below. Chest and legs darker brown. Tail moderately long, tufted or fringed at tip. In East Africa roan are rather more rufous-tinted than the greyer South African specimens. Hair on throat so long as to be almost bearded. A short, ridged, darker mane extends down back of neck to withers. Calves light fawn, facial markings less distinct. Sexes alike, though the markings in bulls are darker than on the cows.

Horns.—Present in both sexes, larger and stouter in bulls. In young animals the short horns are less noticeable than the very long ears. The horns, boldly ridged, are curved backwards, but are less imposing and much shorter than those of Sable. In Kenya, they measure up to 29 inches in a very good bull—cow, horns less.

Distribution.—Roan are now very locally distributed in Kenya. The Mara National Reserve alone (in 1955 a small herd of Roan Antelope was seen on the Chyulu Hills—Tsavo National Park (West)) contains them among the present Kenya National Parks and National Reserves, and here they are fortunately relatively common in small herds. Elsewhere they have been described from the Masai Reserve and Southern Kavirondo district.

Habits.—Although not as imposing or majestic in appearance as the black and white Sable antelope with its greater, more boldly backward-curved horns, the Roan, by reason of his greater size and almost perfect proportions, is certainly one of the finest of African antelopes. He is also one of the most widely distributed throughout Africa south of the Sahara, occurring in almost every territory (though locally) except in the forested areas. In Kenya his range has become more restricted than it was formerly.

In colouration, Roan somewhat resemble waterbuck but the contrasting black and white of the face, and long pointed ears, are easy identification marks. Roan are principally *grazers*, but they occasionally browse on certain shrubs. They are usually found in small troops of from half a dozen to a dozen or fifteen, but as many as thirty together have been recorded. They quite often associate with eland—liking rather similar open or lightly wooded country—and sometimes may be seen with wildebeest or zebra. They are said never to associate with their kinsmen —the Sable—though where both occur the two species mingle at waterholes.

Roan antelopes walk at a rather stately, dignified gait; and gallop fast when alarmed. They carry their heads rather more horizontally than do sable, and consequently lack the proud bearing of the slightly shorter sable who arches his neck.

Roan antelopes are highly courageous, and charge savagely when wounded. Lions have a great respect for both Roan and sable, and certainly seem to attack them less than they do the other antelope, and are not infrequently seriously injured, even occasionally fatally, during such attacks. The usual sound emitted by Roan is an equine snort, when alarmed; but when fighting they squeal with anger, and a wounded one is said to make hissing sounds.

The calves are a light fawn in colour, with the typical long ears but less distinct eye-tufts and facial markings. They are born just before the rains, and the gestation period is about 9 months (Pitman).

Spoor.—Bluntly heart-shaped; similar to but larger and more heavily imprinted than that of sable.

EAST AFRICAN SABLE ANTELOPE

Hippotragus niger roosevelti (Heller)

(Kiswahili : *Pala hala*)

Field Impression.—Black, with snow-white underparts and white face markings. Stout, boldly backward-curved horns. Heavy mane on back of neck. Cows are more rufous-chestnut above.

Descriptive Notes.—The Sable antelope stands rather less at the shoulder than his cousin the Roan, but is more compactly built. A bull and a cow have been recorded at 54 inches and 53¼ inches at the shoulder respectively. Weight of a bull approximately 500 lbs. Adult bulls are dark, rich brown (almost black) above, and pure white below, including the inner sides of the legs as far as knee and hock. The lower part of the rump, round the tail, is also white. There are white tufts in front of the eyes, prolonged into white streaks along the side of the muzzle, and the forepart of cheeks, throat and chin is white. Ears narrow and pointed, fringed with white in front, rufous behind. Forehead and upper part of muzzle dark brown or black in bulls, more rufous-tinged in cows. *The cows are similarly coloured to the bulls, but more chestnut-tinged above in East Africa.* Calves light fawn, but with facial markings indicated. The hair of the coat is finer, and more silky, than that of the Roan. A very thick, partially-drooping, mane of black hairs extends along back of neck to just beyond the withers. *Tail,* moderately long,

41

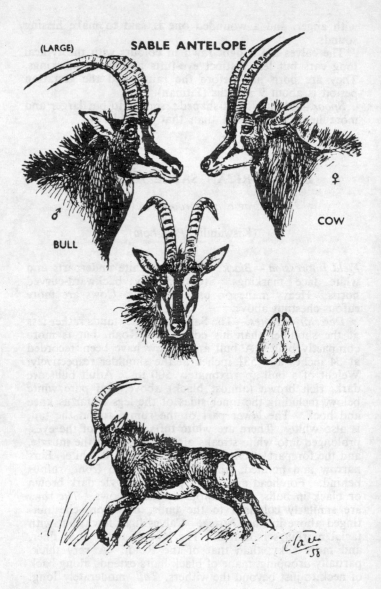

SABLE ANTELOPE

(LARGE)

♂
BULL

♀
COW

fringed at side and tufted : black above, white below.

Horns.—Present in both sexes. The East African Sable antelope is a smaller beast, and carries similar horns, than the South African Sable. The record length is only 40 inches: the average length of the male horns in this race being, according to Lydekker, about 32 inches. South African bull horns average 38-40 inches along curve; average length of cow horns about 30 inches (the "Giant" Sable of Angola (*H. n. Variani*) bears horns measuring up to 64¾ inches in length). In bulls, the horns grow upwards and sweep over backwards in a magnificent curve. They are somewhat flattened laterally, and are thickly ringed to within a few inches of the points. The horns of cows are more slender and less backward curved, but very sharp.

Distribution.—The East African race marks the northen-most extremity of the Sable, and it is "confined to the coastal zone and the immediately adjacent hinterland" (Ritchie). It is unfortunately not represented in any present National Park, or National Reserve, of Kenya. Blayney-Percival gives the habitat as the "extreme South-easterly corner of the Protectorate". The type is recorded from the Shimba Hills, Kwale District, Kenya Colony (1910).

Habits.—The Sable Antelope is gregarious, runnning in herds which generally number from about 10 to 40 or 50 individuals. From 10—20 seems to be the average size of Sable herds, and bulls may be seen in small groups, pairs, or solitary. When alarmed, a Sable herd gallops off in a compact "troop" : that of roan antelopes usually canters away in single file. In many ways the two species are similar in habits, though Sable inhabit rather more densely wooded country by preference. Both are *grazers*, and both drink regularly, and are never found very far from water, and are migratory during dry periods. Like the roan, the Sable is a formidable fighter, and when seriously wounded it will lie down, and sweep viciously from side to side with its sabre-like horns. Lions have been killed when injudiciously attacking a Sable bull. Sable may sometimes be seen in company with herds of wildebeest, zebra, ostrich, etc., though they do not as a rule associate with roan. The only sound I have heard them utter is a horse-like snort.

THE ORYXES

(LARGE)

BEISA

FRINGE-EARED
ORYX

FRINGE-EARED
ORYX

BEISA

44

Its practice of holding its head with neck rather arched—both when walking and galloping—imparts to the Sable a haughty, dignified appearance which is not possessed to the same extent by any other antelope. The calves are born at the beginning of the rainy season, and the period of gestation is about 170 days.

BEISA

Oryx beisa annectens (Hollister)

(Kiswahili : *Choroa*)

Field Impression.—A pale reddish-grey antelope with black and white marked face; black lateral band, and long, narrow straight-back rapier horns. Long black tuft to tail. Ears narrow and pointed with *no tufts of hair at tips*. *Slight* ridged mane along back of neck.

Descriptive Notes.—The Beisa Oryx is a lighter built animal than the South African Gemsbok; the horns are shorter and not so widespread at the tips, and the tail has a shorter brush at its tip. The relatively broad white eye-stripe is continuous with the white of the muzzle, whereas in the Gemsbok the blackish-brown middle and lateral face streaks are connected short of the muzzle. There is no throat tuft, and no black markings on buttocks or thighs. There is a black band round the foreleg just above the knee, and the front of the knee, and a patch on the foreleg is black. The whole of the upper parts (apart from a short dark dorsal stripe), including the neck are rufous-grey—greyer in tint than in the Fringe-eared Oryx. Underparts white. Black tuft of tail reaches to just below hocks. *Weight*, about 450 lbs. Light markings on face and limbs white.

Horns.—Present in both sexes. Long, straight back from the head, narrow and rapier-like, and ringed to within a few inches of the pointed tips. They grow longer in the cows. The longest bull horns measured 38 inches; the longest cow horns 40½ inches.

Distribution.—From Eritrea, through Abyssinia to Somaliland, as far south as the Taba River in Kenya. Westwards to the Laikipia plateau and N.E. Karamoja. Of the Kenya National Parks and National Reserves, only the Marsabit N.R. has the Beisa and there it is plentiful.

Habits.—Beisa are gregarious; running in herds of from half a dozen to fifty individuals, chiefly composed of cows and calves. Old bulls frequently lead a solitary existence. They prefer fairly open, scrub-covered plains, and are shy and wary by nature. They often associate with Grévy's zebra, and are grazers. Oryx are said to be less dependent on water than any other East African antelope, and are often found in the driest areas. The bulls are massive, tough creatures : the skin of the top of the shoulder is so thick that it is greatly prized by the Somalis for making into fighting shields. Many a lion has been fatally injured by the vicious thrust of an Oryx's horns, and the bulls fight savagely during the rutting season.

The young are said to be born between January and March.

FRINGE-EARED ORYX

Oryx beisa callotis (Thomas)

(Kiswahili : *Choroa.* Masai : *Olgomoszorok*)

Field Impression.—Similar in general appearance to Beisa, but the *tips of its ears are fringed with black hairs*, and these tufts are quite conspicuous. General body hue rather more rufous than the greyer Beisa. No black on forelegs below knees.

Descriptive Notes.—This race is said to grow slightly shorter horns than the typical Beisa. The light markings on the face are of a fawner tone, and the dark eye-stripe is extended to the lower jaw. It is decidedly of a more rufous tint on the upper parts. Height and weight about the same as for Beisa.

Horns.—Present in both sexes, similar to those in Beisa, but averaging slightly shorter. Record cow horns 39 inches.

Distribution.—From south-east of Tana river to the Kilimanjaro region, thence into Tanganyika. Ranging west into the Rift Valley. It is fairly common in Amboseli National Reserve, and Tsavo National Park (East and West Sections), but does not occur in the Nairobi N.P.; Mara N.R.; or the Mountain National Parks. Its place in Marsabit is taken by the Beisa.

Habits.—Similar to those of Beisa, though Fringe-eared oryx seem to occur in rather denser, thorny-bush areas than do Beisa. They may easily be seen in the Amboseli and Tsavo areas and, like Beisa, they are shy, wary antelope which soon take to flight when the visitor halts to look at them. As they gallop away, the long bushy tails are swung from side to side, as in wildebeest. The conspicuous tufts at the tips of the ears are most noticeable; and the attitude and form of the ears are very much like those of Roan antelope. They wander in herds from five to about thirty-five individuals, and the old bulls sometimes dwell alone, or in pairs, etc.

GREATER KUDU

Tragelaphus strepsiceros frommi (Matschie)

(Kiswahili : *Tandala kubwa*)

Field Impression.—Very large, but lightly built grey or fawn antelope with several vertical white stripes on body, great wide-spreading spiralled horns (males only); heavy throat and neck beard (males); humped shoulder, shortish bushy tail, and enormously broad ears.

Descriptive Notes.—Bulls measure up to nearly 5 feet at the shoulder, with a weight of over 500 lbs. (705 lbs. has been recorded). General body colour greyish-fawn (old bulls are always greyer than the cows); becoming tan on upper legs, below knees whitish. A number of vertical

GREATER KUDU

(LARGE)

BULL ♂

YOUNG BULLS

♀ COW

48

narrow white stripes adorn the body and rump (said to be never more than about eight in the East African kudu), and there is a broad white chevron between the eyes, and one or two white spots on the cheeks (sometimes merged into a "bar"). Chin and sides ot upper lip white. A heavy brown and white beard adorns throat, extended in the form of a heavy, impressive neck fringe as far as the chest. A narrow mane extends down back of neck, continuing in the form of a white ridge of long hairs along the back to the tail, which is about a foot long, narrow and bushy, greyish brown above with darker tip, and white below. *Females and young* more rufous-fawn in ground colour : cows have no throat or neck fringe. The ears, in both sexes, are exceedingly large and broad, their pinkish flesh interiors thickly fringed with white hairs. A brown patch marks the hinder part of the foreleg above the knee.

Horns.—In males only. Long, massive, and beautifully spiralled in three full curves—the extreme tips sometimes inclining inwards, sometimes outwards. The horns are smoothly ridged, and fluted on outer edge. In young bulls they grow first upwards and outwards. The East African Kudu average shorter horns than those from South Africa, and the record appears to be 58¼ inches along outside curve, and 41¼ inches in a straight line (for Kenya). Tanganyika has produced a 63½ inch head (along curves), and in South Africa, 71½ inches along outside curves has been recorded from the Transvaal.

Distribution.—The greater kudu is one of the rarest and most locally distributed of the antelopes of East Africa. In Kenya it is "as a whole confined to isolated and widely separated localities" (Guggisberg). So far as the Kenya National Parks and Reserves are concerned, it has been reported from Ol Doinyo Orok, in the Amboseli N.R.; and occurs only in the Western section of Tsavo N.P., where it is "very rare" in the Chuylu mountains and on Mungai. It is best represented in the Marsabit National Reserve, where it is quite common, and easily seen. It does not exist in either the Nairobi N.P., or the Mara N.R., nor is it found in the Mountain National Parks.

Habits.—Greater Kudu associate in small herds which average from about six to twenty animals; such herds usually consisting of cows, calves, and young bulls—with sometimes a large bull in attendance. The big bulls usually dwell apart from the cows, only joining them for breeding purposes. They may be seen in troops up to eight or ten, very often of different ages; and very big old bulls are often solitary. They are principally *browsing* animals, eating leaves, shoots and wild fruits, but also graze young grass. They are usually found in hilly, broken and stony, and often fairly densely bushed country, and seem to be fairly independent of water, though drinking regularly where such is present. The call is a loud, hoarse bark. When alarmed, and cantering away at their rather "rocking-horse" gait, Kudu curl up their bushy tails over the rump, fanning out the white, bushy underside. When galloping through very dense bush, the bulls lay their huge, unwieldy horns right back along their shoulders. The calves are born at the beginning of the rains : gestation period 7-8 months. Male Kudu are seldom attacked unless by lions, but cows and young are attacked by leopard, cheetah and wild dogs.

THE WATERBUCK

1. COMMON RINGED WATERBUCK

Kobus ellipsiprymnus thikae (Matschie)
Kobus ellipsiprymnus kuro (Heller)

(Kiswahili : *Kuro*)

Field Impression.—Robust, thickset antelopes with wiry, rough coats : brownish-grey *with white ring round rump.* Shaggy hair round throat, and horns (males only) ruggedly ringed, curved backwards, outwards and upwards. Tail only moderate, skimpily fringed at tip.

2. KENYA DEFASSA WATERBUCK

Kobus defassa raineyi (Heller)

Field Impression.—Similar in build, horns, etc., to above, but with *white patch on inner sides of rump.* Rather more rufous in tinge generally above.

Descriptive Notes for both.—Shoulder height in bulls of both species 48-54 inches. Weight : 395 lbs. (*Defassa*—East Africa) : 475 lbs. (*Ellipsiprymnus*—Lyell). Waterbuck are large, heavy creatures, with shaggy coats. The common type is on the whole greyer or browner than the Defassa which is markedly more rufous-tinted above, with decidedly darker legs. Both have a white ruff round the throat and conspicuous white marks above the eyes, and white round nose and chin. Whereas the Common Waterbuck has a white band round each buttock (forming

THE WATERBUCK

(LARGE)

♂ BULL

♀ COW

DEFASSA

RINGED WATERBUCK

a "ring"), the Defassa has entirely white buttocks from the root of the tail to the hocks.

Horns.—In males only. Very symmetrical, massive at base, deeply annulated, and extending evenly backwards, outwards, upwards and finally curving gently forwards : some having a very wide spread from tip to tip, others a very narrow one. The Kenya record for *Ellipsiprymnus* is just over 31 inches, and for *Defassa* just under 33 inches. The Uganda *Defassa* carry the finest heads in Africa. In young bulls the horns first grow upwards and outwards.

Distribution.—The *common ringed waterbuck* to-day ranges from Zululand, through eastern Africa, to Southern Abyssinia and Somalia, including Bechuanaland and Ngamiland. The *Defassa* inhabits more upland country; is found in Angola and extreme north-west of South-West Africa, ranging from Belgian Congo, Northern Rhodesia, Nyasaland and Portuguese East Africa through East Africa and the Sudan and Abyssinia, thence westwards into West Africa (Pitman).

Both *Defassa* and *Ellipsiprymnus* occur in the Nairobi National Park, where they can be compared with interest. It is the only known part of Africa where the two species interbreed, and variations of the distinctive markings from one extreme to the other can easily be seen there. *Defassa* are also common in Mara National Reserve and in the Aberdares but do not occur in any of the other Kenya National Parks or National Reserves. *Ellipsiprymnus*, on the other hand, is plentiful in Marsabit N.R.; and in Tsavo N.P. (both east and west sections), also Amboseli N.R., where it is not plentiful.

Habits.—The habits of both species are similar, though the Defassa is stated to confine itself more closely to the actual neighbourhood of water than does the common species. Both are good swimmers, and do not hesitate to take refuge from enemies such as wild dogs by submerging their bodies in some deep pool. Waterbuck are gregarious, herding in troops of from about twelve to thirty : for the most part consisting of cows and young animals and calves, with a mature herd bull. Bulls, in small groups of four to six, are often seen together, and, as with some other game, old bulls are often solitary.

WHITE-BEARDED GNU (WILDEBEEST)

COW ♀

BULL ♂

YOUNG

They are sociable creatures, and often mix with impala, wildebeest, etc. Waterbuck are plentiful in river valleys, and areas of long, lush grass, more or less thickly wooded, and they are also found in broken, stony country—but never very far from water. They are not so truly swamp-dwellers as Lechwe or Sitatunga.

Waterbuck are preyed upon by lions, and the females and young by leopard, cheetah, and wild dogs. They exude a characteristic, strong, turpentine-like odour.

KENYA WHITE-BEARDED WILDEBEEST or GNU

Connochaetes taurinus albojubatus (Thomas)

(Kiswahili : *Nyumbu*)

Field Impression.—A rather hump-backed antelope with "cow-like" horns, "horse-like" black mane and tail, and white beard. Dull grey, with darker vertical stripes along forepart of body. Face black.

Descriptive Notes.—Although the Wildebeeste, or Gnus, are sometimes popularly believed to belong to the ox group, they are, of course, in reality antelopes, related to the Hartebeest. The Blue Wildebeest, or Brindled Gnu, is widely spread throughout Africa from the Orange River to Central Kenya, varying in several local subspecies, of which that in Kenya and Northern Tanganyika is distinguished principally by its white, or pale yellowish, throat-beard. In other respects it is a paler, more evenly-coloured beast than the southern types of Blue Wildebeest : noticeably so in the legs which in East Africa are con-colorous with the rest of the body, merely becoming slightly paler : whereas in the southern races the legs are a decided tan hue. The somewhat irregular and rather broad trans-verse stripes or streaks along the neck and the body are less well-marked in *Albojubatus* than in the typical Blue Wildebeest, where they are stronger and darker, often decidedly redder-tinted.

55

Forepart of face black, with coarse, tufted hair. There is a large, raised glandular patch below the eye. Nostrils very broad. Tail fringed at sides and ending in a long black brush, reaching just below the hocks. A partially drooping mane of long black hairs (sometimes mingled with a few white ones) extends along back of neck to withers : the hair being forward-directed as far as the shoulders, then falling backwards. Calves are light fawn, with dark dorsal line. Height at shoulder 52 inches; weight about 550 lbs.

Horns.—Present in both sexes, but more massive and widely curved in bulls. Black, smooth and curving slightly upwards then downwards and outwards : the tips inclining forwards. In young animals the horns at first grow straight upwards and begin as projecting points. The maximum horn span for East Africa is just over 30 inches.

Distribution.—Very numerous in the Nairobi National Park, and in the Amboseli National Reserve. Wildebeest only occur in the neighbourhood of Campi ya Simba and Marabu in the Western section of Tsavo N.P. They are not recorded from the Eastern section of the Tsavo Park or Mara. They do not occur at Marsabit N.R.

Habits.—Wildebeest are gregarious and very sociable and are among the most typical of the "Plains" game. They frequently associate with Burchell's zebras, Topi or Hartebeest, ostriches and the plains' gazelle, etc., but for some, at present, mysterious reason their habitat seems to be more restricted in East Africa than that of the other plains' animals. They are therefore more locally distributed than one would expect. Where they do occur, they are always exceedingly plentiful, and this is especially so in the Royal Nairobi National Park where they are very tame. They are essentially grass-eaters, and always dependent on regular water supply, so they are prone to great annual migrations when many thousands of them combine to form—in places like the Serengeti Plains of Tanganyika—a most wonderful spectacle.

Calving begins as a rule during the first week in March, and is usually finished by the end of April.

In spite of their odd, grotesque appearance, Wildebeest are playful creatures, and in the early mornings in particular, delight to play frolicking games of "follow my leader," cantering round in circles with much violent shieing and plunging and whisking of tails. At such times the herd bulls can be heard making the sonorous bleating grunt which sounds like *"Kwang"*—repeated several times in succession. A herd walks, or gallops, in single file : and when a large herd is following a game trail to a favoured drinking place, it can be spread out over a long distance. The body tends to slope back from the shoulders, and the massive head is carried low. When alarmed, Wildebeest at first stand gazing, with heads raised and ears widespread, in the direction from which the supposed danger threatens. They have a rather stupid habit of blowing loudly through their nostrils on such occasions (producing a loud "sshwaa"), which always betrays them easily to a human hunter. They are very inquisitive, and will stand thus for some time before suddenly, with one accord, wheeling about and prancing away—at their curious hunched gallop—with wildly whisking tails. Unless very seriously alarmed (or where much persecuted) they seldom go far before halting to turn and stand once more, with the usual loud wheezy snorts, before retreating again, and so on.

The adult Wildebeest is a powerful, robust animal; thoroughly courageous in defence. Only the lion will tackle an adult bull or cow; and although Wildebeest form a very common prey of lions, wherever the former are plentiful, there are several instances on record where a bull Wildebeest has beaten off a young lion and chased him ignominiously away! When fighting, two bulls drop down on their knees and clash their heads together with a violence that one would suppose should shatter their skulls! The calves are delightful little creatures with their silky fawn coats and frizzy tails, and they bleat and "moo" very like domestic calves.

Wildebeest are very fond of rolling in dust, and such shallow "wallows", surrounded by the usual clusters and heaps of the "top" shaped droppings, are common features of country they inhabit; and, incidentally, assist to conserve water during heavy rains.

The spoor is broad at base, tapering to a fairly sharp point, and is very characteristic.

(LARGE)

YOUNG

COKE'S HARTEBEEST
OR "KONGONI"

COKE'S HARTEBEEST (KONGONI)

Alcelaphus buselaphus cokei (Gunther)

(Kiswahili : *Kongoni*)

Field Impression.—A long-faced, dark fawn-coloured antelope, paling to whitish on rump : with humped shoulder and horns rising from a bony pedicle at back of head. Horns appear bracket-shaped when seen from front Z-shaped when viewed from the side.

Descriptive Notes.—Shoulder height approximately 4 feet. There is a decided slope of the back from shoulders to rump. General colour is a darker or lighter sandy-fawn above : darker on back, becoming paler on legs and underparts and almost white on rump. Face brown, very long and narrow, with rather wild, goat-like eyes. Tail not very long, fringed with dark brown or black, and tufted. Ears narrow and pointed. Sexes alike, and small calves are light fawn. One gets the impression that Kongoni in the Tsavo National Park are rather redder in tone above than those in Nairobi area. Weight about 312 lbs.

Horns.—Present in both sexes, and relatively short and thick. Well ridged, with sharply-pointed, backward-extending tips. They grow outwards from the pedicle, shortly upwards, and sharply backwards; and are more massive in bulls than in cows. Record male horn length is 21 inches along the curve. In young animals the horns at first grow upwards in points.

Distribution.—Very numerous in Nairobi National Park. It is common in Tsavo N.P. (east and west). It does not occur at Marsabit, but has been recorded at Amboselik. It occurs at Mara.

Habits.—The Kongoni is a grazer and a lover of the open plains, though often found in dry, thorny-bush-scrub as long as there is plenty of grass. They associate in small herds, and are always very alert, usually having one cow acting as sentry while the others graze. Although now greatly restricted in range, the Kongoni was at one time the most plentiful of the Plains' antelopes of Kenya.

Like all of the hartebeest, the Kongoni can move very fast when he wants to, and, when galloping all out at his deceptive, hunched gait—with head and neck well forward—it is said to take a good horse to keep up with him. The sharp "cough-like" snort uttered when alarmed, or suspicious, seems to be the only sound associated with Coke's Hartebeest.

Kongoni, like wildebeest, are frequently found in the company of other antelopes, zebras and ostriches, etc. Like wildebeest, too, they are greatly troubled with a species of "Bot" fly, the broad, flat *grubs* of which manage, somehow, to get right up into the animal's nasal cavities. This is said to be the cause of the constant tossing and shaking of the head, accompanied by sneezing, and also of the grotesque prancing about to which both these antelopes are prone. The young are born at the beginning of the rains.

Kongoni are much preyed upon by lions, and wild dogs are serious enemies as well.

JACKSON'S HARTEBEEST

Alcelaphus buselaphus jacksoni (Thomas)

(Kiswahili : *Kongoni*)

Field Impression.—Typical hartebeest form, with humped shoulder, sloping back, and very long face : but horns mounted on very high pedicle : forming a narrow "V" in front view; and continued almost in line of face backwards, upwards, and strongly .projecting back at points. Colour a uniform, bright rufous.

Descriptive Notes.—Height about 4 feet 4 inches at shoulder. Weight about 405 lbs. Jackson's Hartebeest is a larger animal than the Kongoni. It has a longer face, and a higher pedicle, and the horns have a narrow spread, rising steeply upwards, then backwards, as in the Cape Hartebeest. It is a bright, foxy-red colour; with no black markings on face or legs. Sexes alike.

(LARGE)

KENYA JACKSON'S HARTEBEEST

HUNTER'S HARTEBEEST OR HIROLA

61

Horns.—As described above, strongly ridged in front. the record horn length is 26 inches, with the horn tips 14⅞ inches apart. Female horns more slender.

Distribution.—Jackson's Hartebeest has a more limited range than Coke's Hartebeest, and does not occur in the Nairobi N.P. It is plentiful, in small herds, in the Mara N.R. In Marsabit National Reserve it is very localised, and comparatively few in numbers. Some 2-300 of these hartebeest live on Leroghi, and are usually to be seen in the Bawa valley and on the Veterinary Quarantine near Kisima.

Habits.—Very similar to those of the Kongoni : preferring fairly open country with short grass. Bulls, or old cows, often take up sentry positions on anthills. Like Coke's, very fast when at full gallop : and also gallops with head forward. On the rolling grassy downs of the Mau plateau they were formerly very common from about 5,000 to 8,000 feet. "Where plentiful they are found in herds of four or five up to forty or fifty and sometimes more, also single bulls by themselves" (Sir F. J. Jackson).

The foxy-red colour, and upright horns, should aid identification and distinction from Coke's Hartebeest.

HUNTER'S HARTEBEEST OR HIROLA

Damaliscus hunteri (Sclater)

Field Impression.—Hartebeest-like form, but with less "humped" withers, and horns shaped rather like those of impala. Rufous-fawn, with distinct white chevron on forehead. Lower half of tail white.

Descriptive Notes.—Shoulder height about 48 inches. The general colour is rufous-fawn, and across the forehead is an upward-directed, very narrow white chevron. This antelope belongs to the *Damaliscus* group (containing the Topi, Tiang, Korrigum, Tssessebe, Blesbuck and Bontebok) which, though closely related to the true hartebeest, differs from them in having a rather shorter face, absence of a distinct horn pedicle, and no sudden angulation in the horns themselves—which generally form a simple curve. Ears and face narrow and prolonged. Lower half of tail white.

Horns.—Present in both sexes. Heavily ridged, and shaped very like those of impala. Maximum length $26\frac{3}{4}$ inches, good average specimens running up to about 25 or 26 inches.

Distribution.—One of the most localised of the African antelopes and restricted in range to the neighbourhood of the Tana river in Kenya and neighbouring Somalia. According to Captain A. T. A. Ritchie (writing in 1932), "they inhabit a zone some sixty miles broad north of the Tana river, which is, roughly, as follows : from about Massa Bubu on the Tana, downstream to within some forty miles of the coast, the zone runs for about one hundred and twenty miles, first north-easterly and then northward. Within this area they are fairly numerous."

Habits.—According to Captain Ritchie, Hunter's Hartebeest run in herds from half a dozen to forty, though it is uncommon to see more than twenty together. The sexes evidently dwell apart for most of the year : male herds consisting of old and young animals, and female herds, containing a number of young males, with one large bull in charge. They prefer open, dry, plain country, but are often seen in broken thorn bush and occasionally in very dense bush country. They are very wary and difficult to approach, and often seek the company of Oryx or Topi. Like Coke's and Jackson's Hartebeest, Hunter's hartebeest frequently mount sentry duty on anthills or hillocks.

TOPI

Damaliscus korrigum (Ogilby)

(Kiswahili: *Nyamera*)

Field Impression.—A hartebeest-like antelope with fairly short but stout, ridged horns which curve regularly backwards, with only the short tips recurving upwards. Rich

bay or rufous, with black markings on the upper forelegs, hips, and thighs; and a blackish blaze down the face.

Descriptive Notes.—The Topi is a powerful, robust antelope with a shoulder height of some 48 to 50 inches. Like its relatives, the Tiang and the Tssessebe, its coat has a rich plum-like sheen : its bright bay colour reflecting with purplish lights. The black patches on the upper part of forelegs and thighs are conspicuous. The ears are narrow and pointed, and the tail only moderately long and fringed and tufted with black at its extremity. The young are fawn. Weight 300 lbs.

Horns.—Heavily ridged, slightly lyrate, and curving evenly backwards then slightly upwards at the short tips. Present in both sexes, but more massive in bulls. 19¼ inches seems to be the record for Kenya.

Distribution.—Topi are likely to be seen only in Mara National Reserve, of the present Kenya National Parks and National Reserves. Elsewhere, the East African distribution is said to be from Central Tanganyika and the Serengeti Plains westwards to Lakes Kivu and Albert, northwards to Uasin Gishu plateau and northern Uganda, and from Jubaland south along the Kenya coast to the mouth of the Sabaki (Guggisberg). In the Mara N.R. Topi are common.

Habits.—Topi run in herds up to about twenty as a rule, but sometimes very large herds are encountered, especially near Lakes Edward and Albert, and they prefer fairly open plains country, with or without scattered bush, with shortish grass. They are fine-looking beasts, with their reddish colouring and black patches, and slightly lyrate, backward curved horns. They have the same rather hunched, but speedy gallop of the hartebeest tribe, and are the northern representative of the Tssessebe (*D.Lunatus*). They are grazers.

MEDIUM-SIZED ANTELOPES

LESSER KUDU

Tragelaphus imberbis australis (Heller)

(Kiswahili : *Tandala ndogo*)

(Masai : *Osiram*)

Field Impression.—Like a miniature Greater Kudu, except that there is no beard or throat-fringe, and the spiralled horns are shorter in proportion and more narrowly set. White patch on throat and across lower neck. Vertical white stripes slong body more numerous, and ears narrower. Dark grey to yellowish grey; the rams are greyer than the ewes and young animals. Legs tan. Only males have horns.

Descriptive Notes.—Shoulder height about 41 inches, weight about 230 lbs. Blyth named the Lesser Kudu *Imberbis* in recognition of its lack of a throat fringe, one of its conspicuous distinctions from the Greater Kudu. A ram is a most handsome creature with his rich grey colouring, thirteen or fourteen narrow white vertical stripes, conspicuous white patch on throat and white bar across lower neck. There is a short white mane down back of neck, top of shoulders, and along back; and a narrow white chevron between the eyes, and white round the lips. A couple of white spots mark the cheeks, and the forepart of the face (especially the underpart) is almost black. Tail bushy, grey above, but white below, with white tip. Two dark patches occur on the legs, above knee and hock respectively, and the legs below these points are tan. Females more fawn-grey than old rams; but similarly marked. Ears, white-fringed, are noticeably narrower than those of Greater Kudu.

Horns.—In Kenya average about 30-31 inches. In males only. Record lengths are 35¼ inches and 36 inches. Like those of Greater Kudu, the horns grow in three spirals, but are more slender and more narrowly set.

(MEDIUM) **LESSER KUDU**

RAM ♂

EWE ♀

Distribution.—Marsabit National Reserve : Amboseli National Reserve : Royal Tsavo National Park (East and West sections). It is common and easily seen in the above areas, but is not present in Nairobi National Park, nor in the Mara N.R.

Habits.—Lesser Kudu like the drier, thorny-bush areas where, during the heat of the day, they lie up in thickets or clumps of bushy growth—feeding and moving about during the night, early mornings, and late afternoons. One is greatly struck with the resemblance to Greater Kudu in their actions and gait. They adopt the same rocking-horse-like gallop, with bushy tails fanned and upward curled behind—revealing the bobbing white underpart, as they bound through the scrub of their typical dry, thorny "*Nyika*" surroundings. A similar, though less deep, coughing bark is uttered by both sexes.

Lesser Kudu associate in small herds, ranging from pairs to four or six—the latter probably consisting of a ram and five ewes. Old rams often lead solitary lives, while 4-6 rams of varying ages may sometimes be seen together. Like his greater cousin, the Lesser Kudu is principally a browsing antelope : feeding on various leaves, seedpods, wild fruits, and so on. C. G. Schillings states that they feed largely upon the rigid, spiky *Sanseviera* known as "Bowstring hemp", and that he found their stomachs sometimes completely filled with the long fibres.

Their principal natural enemies seem to be leopard and wild dog.

For a good chance of seeing Lesser Kudu, one should get into a suitable area as early in the morning as possible, or in the late afternoon.

SITUTUNGA

Tragelaphus spekei spekei Sclater

(Kiswahili : *Nzohe*)

Field Impression.—Somewhat resembles a bushbuck, but larger, with coarse, wiry hair, and curiously narrow,

SITUTUNGA

EWE

RAM

elongated hooves. Greyish brown on upper parts in males, more rufous in females. Horns longer and more twisted than those of bushbuck or nyala. White chevron between the eyes.

Descriptive Notes.—Shoulder height 43-48 inches. Males grey-brown in body colour, rufous-brown in females. Both sexes have a white chevron between the eyes, white patches on lower neck and throat, and a few white spots or stripes on haunches and flanks—the latter often faint or absent in old rams. The coat is long and wiry. The lateral hooves are relatively large, and the main hooves (both fore and hind) exceptionally long and narrow, to enable the animal to walk over marshy ground, swampy mud, etc. Space between false hooves and true hooves devoid of hair (as in another swamp-dweller, the Lechwe). Ears rather short and broad, with fringes of white hair on inner margin. Tail short and slender, brown above and white below. Weight 200-250 lbs.

Horns.—Males only. Very long and beautifully twisted, they wear yellowish at the tips. Up to 36⅜ inches.

Distribution.—The Situtunga has a greatly restricted range in Kenya. "In the Trans Nzoia district, where the local authorities have taken steps to create a Nature Reserve on part of Mount Elgon, a group of landowners have, in the most praiseworthy way, instituted a small but successful Situtunga sanctuary on their own land. This is one of the few places in Kenya where these rare animals can be found, and where they can be observed and photographed at close quarters. Had it not been for the enthusiasm of these farmers there is little doubt that few, if any, of the Situtunga would have survived. This small sanctuary will now be afforded adequate protection". (1956 *Report : Kenya Wild Life Society*).

Habits.—The Situtunga, or Marsh Antelope, inhabits dense reedbeds or papyrus swamps, and its range is entirely restricted to such a habitat. It is a wary, shy creature which rarely issues from the dense swamp vegetation, and little has been recorded of its habits. Captain Pitman has recorded that it will interbreed freely with the closely related bushbuck in captivity. In Ngamiland it is said to come out into the fringes of the swamp vegetation during the very hottest hours of the day (Cronje Wilmot), but as a

70

rule Situtunga only issue into the open after dark. They are strong swimmers, and when alarmed submerge their bodies entirely, exposing only the nostrils above water. The bark, which is uttered by both sexes, is described as rather "muffled"—not unlike the grunt of a pig.

Owing to the peculiarly long and narrow hooves, the spoor is easily recognisable, forming a long V-shaped track. Pitman records that numerous juveniles were observed on April 9th (1927) on Nkose Island (Lake Victoria), some only just dropped and the size of tiny kids.

Leopard, and possibly crocodile are probably their principal natural enemies. Python may take the young inside papyrus swamps.

IMPALA

Aepyceros melampus suara (Matschie)

(Kiswahili : *Swala Pala*)

Field Impression.—Very gracefully built, rufous-fawn above (darker, with a clear horizontal line of demarcation along upper part of body), paling to lighter fawn on flanks, white on abdomen. Horns, in males, gracefully lyrate, ridged. A black stripe borders white rump on each side below tail. Tail moderately long and narrow, black, with white border and underpart, and brushy tip.

Descriptive Notes.—The Impala in East Africa grows larger, and has much longer horns, than those in South Africa. It is the most graceful of the antelopes, and its warm rufous-fawn colouring, white underparts, and black and white markings on rump and tail easily distinguish it. Characteristic features are the black tufts or brushes of hair sprouting just above the heel of the hind leg, and these conceal a scent gland. A similar, but bare, black patch is on the flank, just in the angle where it is met by the thigh. There are white streaks in front of the large, lustrous dark eyes, and the chin, and the area round lips, are white. There are faint indications of darker "gazelle" markings

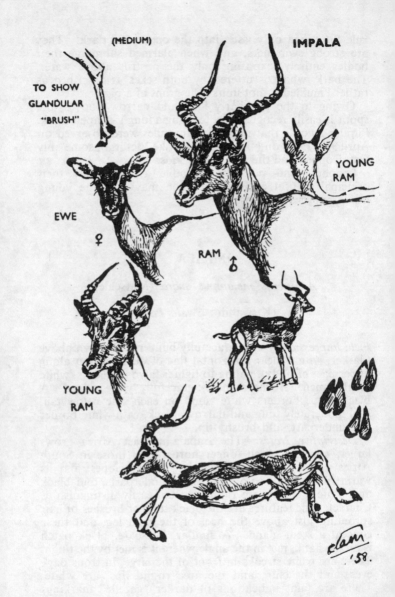

TO SHOW
GLANDULAR
"BRUSH"

(MEDIUM)

IMPALA

YOUNG
RAM

EWE
♀

RAM
♂

YOUNG
RAM

Clam
'58.

running from front corner of eye to nostril. Ears rather narrow; white with black tips. Tail moderately long and narrow; black above, fringed and tufted with white at tip and white on undersurface. A prominent black streak on either side of white rump marking below tail. Height 34-38 inches. Weight 65-70 lbs.

Horns.—In males only. Beautifully and gracefully curved in a wide lyre-shape, inclining upwards and slightly inwards or outwards at tips, which are smooth. The greater part of the horns is ridged in front. In young rams the horns begin as backward-curved spikes; gradually assuming the lyrate form of adulthood. Kenya impala grow the finest heads in Africa. Up to 33 inches along curve. Average between 29 and 30 inches.

Distribution.—One of the most widely distributed East African antelopes : very plentiful in Nairobi National Park; Amboseli National Reserve; Tsavo N.P. (East and West); Mara N.R.; and Marsabit N.R. Not being a forest dweller, it is not found in Mount Kenya or Aberdare National Parks.

Habits.—Impala both browse and graze, and so are plentiful almost everywhere except in mountain forests or in very dry, waterless areas—as they are regular drinkers. In East Africa they seem to be equally well at home in open plains' country, dotted with scrubby bush, or in thick thorny savanna, though in South Africa they definitely prefer Bush veld, the thornier the better—but never far from water of some sort. They usually move in herds of from about ten to fifty animals : such herds usually having one big ram, and several younger ones among the preponderating number of ewes and young. At certain seasons rams dwell together : and at the rutting season rival rams fight furiously, chasing each other about with a succession of loud, guttural grunts reminiscent of some carnivorous animal. In the breeding season the rams may be seen running amorously after the ewes, their white-fringed tails spread fanwise over their rumps, revealing the white undersurface.

Impala are always intensely alert, and the high-pitched, "sneezing" snort of alarm (not unlike, on a smaller scale, that of the Rhinoceros) is the signal for the rapid departure of the herd in a series of the most beautiful leaps and bounds.

CHOBE BUSH BUCK

EWE

RAM

The Impala is the finest jumper in Africa—far better than the famed Springbok of South Africa—and Colonel Stevenson-Hamilton has recorded a jump (with effortless ease) of a little over ten feet : "and the same jump cleared in length over thirty feet".

The single young one is born at the beginning of the rains. Leopard and Cheetah, and especially the Wild Hunting Dog, are the principal natural foes of the Impala. The spoor is neat and pointed and easily recognisable.

BUSHBUCK

Tragelaphus scriptus delamerei (Pocock)

(Kiswahili : *Pongo*)

Field Impression.—Male about as large as a goat; dark rufous-brown to almost black : with a few spots on haunches, some often rather faint, white vertical stripes on body, conspicuous white half-collar round base of neck, and dorsal crest of long white and brown hairs. Tail bushy, brown above, white below. Horns short, stout, and very pointed with a lateral ridge and single spiral. Female hornless, a good deal smaller, and decidedly more rufous in body tone, stripes and spots on body more vivid. Dorsal crest small and dark. Coat rather wiry and long, in both sexes. Neck hairs very short.

Descriptive Notes.—Bushbuck vary a great deal locally in tone of body (ranging from dull rufous to almost black) and quantity and variety of body spots and stripes. The hair on the body is coarse and wiry, but that on neck short and velvety : and there is a curious, almost bare "collar" round base of hinder part of neck. The males are always larger and darker and less richly striped or spotted (except when young) than the females. Inner side of legs white, with dark bands on inside knee and inside hock. White patch on throat, and conspicuous white "clerical collar" round front of lower neck. There are usually more or less distinct white marks in front of the eyes. and one or two white spots on the rufous cheeks. Muzzle dark brown, lips and chin white, ears only mediumly large and oval. Tail bushy, as described above. Height at shoulder : rams about 33 inches; ewes about 31 inches. Weight : Male 100-170 lbs. Female about 9? lbs.

Horns.—Present only in males normally, but female bushbuck occasionally develop horns. Very sharp and dagger-like in young rams, sometimes worn short and blunt in old ones : stout at base, slightly spiralled and margined. They average from about 12 to 15 inches : the record being 21⅝ inches (Kenya).

Distribution.—Bushbuck are dwellers in thickly wooded or forest country, or the thickly bushed margins of streams or rivers and are never found far from covert of some sort. They occur in such wooded areas of Nairobi National Park, Tsavo N.P. (East and West), Mount Kenya and Aberdare Forest National Parks, Amboseli National Reserve, Marsabit N.R., and in Mara N.R., and in many other suitable localities throughout the Territory.

Habits.—Bushbuck are solitary creatures, rarely being seen in greater numbers than pairs, or ram, doe and young one. Old rams frequently lead a solitary existence, and once they become attached to a certain locality, and are undisturbed there, rarely wander far. The presence of water is essential, and there must be plenty of cover and dense undergrowth. They are mainly browsers, eating leaves, shoots, wild fruits, acacia pods, and so on, but also eat young grass. They are fearfully destructive to garden flowers of all sorts, also to many kinds of crops! Very nocturnal and secretive, bushbuck are as a rule only seen feeding and moving about in the early mornings or late afternoons, except in dull or rainy weather. They are slow runners in the open, and easily caught by dogs (wild or domestic), but in thick undergrowth can move with remarkable ease : plunging through it in a series of easy bounds or jumps, so that the movement of an alarmed bushbuck in such covert is registered by a measured "thump! thump! thump!"

Although comparatively small and sturdy, bushbuck are among the most courageous of antelopes, and a ram will charge with the utmost determination when wounded, or bayed, and many dogs have been killed by them, and not a few hunters very seriously injured. The neck of a ram is characteristically thick and powerful. When galloping away, bushbuck raise the bushy tail, showing the white undersurface—like kudu. The leopard, cheetah and wild dog are their most usual natural foes. The call, in both sexes, is a loud, hoarse bark, usually heard at night.

The spoor is small for the size of the animal; almost oval, and larger in rams; rather more pointed and smaller in ewes.

WARD'S BOHOR REEDBUCK

Redunca redunca wardi (Thomas)

(Kiswahili : *Tohe*)

Field Impression.—Uniform sandy-rufous all over, paling to white below. Tail very bushy, white undersurface. Horns only in males, extending backwards and upwards then rather sharply forwards, ringed at base. Head nicely proportioned, and ears rather long and pointed. Coat rather wiry.

Descriptive Notes.—Front of fore-legs darker than the rest of the sandy-rufous upper parts. Top of muzzle slightly darker, and paler rings round the eyes, which are very large and dark. Under parts white. Sexes alike. Shoulder height about 2 feet 6 inches. Weight about 80 lbs.

Horns.—In males only. Ringed at base, they curve rather sharply forwards : normally seldom more than 8-10 inches. The Record is just under 14 inches.

Distribution.—Ward's Reedbuck is common in Nairobi N.P., and in Amboseli N.R. In Tsavo N.P. it is occasionally seen, but not common. It is common in the Mara N.R. This antelope lives either in swampy surroundings among reeds or papyrus, or in open grassland on the higher altitudes, and it is restricted to such areas accordingly.

THE REEDBUCK

♂
WARD'S
BOHOR
REEDBUCK
RAM

♂
CHANLER'S
MOUNTAIN
REEDBUCK
RAM

♀
EWE

Habits.—Ward's Bohor Reedbuck is usually seen singly, or in pairs. It is akin to the typical Reedbuck (*R. arundinum*) which ranges from South Africa to Tanganyika, but it is a smaller animal with shorter and far more "hooked forward" horns. Its habitat varies from altitudes of 8,000 feet or more, to swamps and reedbeds at quite low levels; but, away from swampy surroundings, it prefers open grasslands.

They may sometimes be seen in small parties of five or six, and when lying down in grass or reeds are hard to see. When disturbed, these reedbuck canter away at a very typical "rocking-hore"-like gait, with their bushy tails fanned out behind; often uttering a series of shrill whistling cries. Their uniform rufous-sandy colouring and short, forward-curved horns (in males) render them easy to identify.

CHANLER'S REEDBUCK

Redunca fulvorufula chanleri (Rothschild)

(Kiswahili : *Tohe*)

Field Impression.—A reedbuck fairly similar in size to, but rather greyer in body tone (sandy thighs and legs) than the previous species. The horns of the males are similarly forward-curved but considerably shorter. Often found in small herds.

Descriptive Notes.—Like the previous species, Chanler's Reedbuck has a curious, more or less circular bare patch of skin just below the ears (characteristic of all the Reedbuck family). It is related to the Mountain Reedbuck of South Africa, but is slightly smaller and rather greyer in body tone. Legs and thighs more sandy suffused. White underparts, with a paler ring round the large eyes. Tail bushy, greyish-sandy above, white below. Shoulder height about 28 inches. Weight about 63 lbs.

Horns.—Short, ringed at base, and sharply curved

GERENUK OR WALLER'S GAZELLE

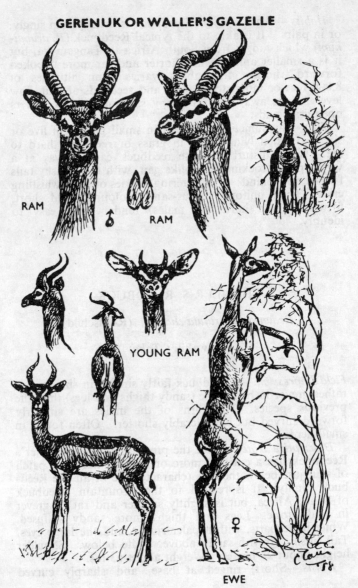

RAM

RAM

YOUNG RAM

EWE

forward (almost hooked) at tips. Record 7 inches : average, about 6½ inches. In males only.

Distribution.—Chanler's reedbuck occur on almost all rough hills of over 4,000 feet throughout the country, except in the Northern District beyond the Uaso Nyiro river (Blayney Percival). In Nairobi N.P. one herd of ten can usually be observed in the Sosian valley, and they are common. They are common locally in Mara west. They are not recorded from Amboseli, nor apparently, from the Tsavo N.P. They are common in the Marsabit N.R.

Habits.—Chanler's Reedbuck is an inhabitant of the hills or hilly country, though it is also sometimes found on the rough slopes of river beds. In hill country, it prefers the grassy slopes and terraces, and, when alarmed, almost invariably seeks safety downhill. These animals often consort in herds of up to fifteen individuals—though usually in smaller lots of from five to eight or so. The females equal, and sometimes exceed, the males in size. The general habits, action in galloping (i.e., legs thrown well outwards fore and aft in typical "rocking-horse" gait), and whistling call resemble those of Ward's Bohor Reedbuck.

GERENUK, OR WALLER'S GAZELLE

Litocranius walleri walleri (Brooke)

(Kiswahili : *Swala twiga*. Masai : *Nanyad*)

Field Impression.—Unmistakable on account of its long neck and rather giraffe-like head—hence popular name "Giraffe-Gazelle." Coloured much like an impala (rufous-fawn above, paler below); the rams with fairly short but well-curved, rather stout, ringed horns. Neck very long, legs long.

Descriptive Notes.—Head rather short, nostrils and upper lip shaped like those of a giraffe. A large, purplish-black glandular patch in front of the eye, which is large and dark. Neck exceptionally long; and colour very like that of an impala (to which it is rather similar in size)—rather dark rufous-fawn above, becoming paler on flanks below a distinct line of demarcation. A white line extends over the top of the eye, and the area round the eye is paler than the rest of the face. Ears fairly long, and rather narrow. Tail remarkably slender and insignificant, moderately long, with a black tuft. Belly, and inner side of limbs, white. Sexes alike. Shoulder height 36-41 inches Weight little over 100 lbs.

Horns.—In males only. Very massive, heavily ridged throughout the greater portion of their extent; widely separated at their bases, and directed at first outwards then forwards, then inwards and backwards—finally bending forwards in somewhat of a hook at the tip. Record horn length is 17 inches. In young, horns first develop as inward-curved spikes.

Distribution.—From Somalia and Southern Abyssinia through Tanaland and the Tsavo region to Kilimanjaro and the Magadi-Natron-Manyara section of the Rift Valley. It is common in Tsavo National Park (East and West); very common at Amboseli; but has not been reported from Mara N.R. One solitary specimen has been seen in the Nairobi Park. It is common at Marsabit. It is relatively common in Ngong N.R.

Habits.—The Gerenuk is certainly one of the strangest creatures in East Africa. It presents a quaint mixture of the grotesque and the graceful, and in form it reminds one of those delicately graceful "blown glass" animals created as ornaments—for which, indeed, it would make an excellent model. The head, very broad between the eyes, tapers narrowly to the wedge-shaped muzzle : and this produces a remarkable illusion when it is facing you at a distance, causing a doubt as to whether you are looking at the front, or the back, of its head! In profile, the pointed muzzle, and the projection of the back of the head behind the ears (which are in themselves inconspicuous at this angle) imparts a curiously snake-like look to the form of the head, and gives the illusion of a definite thickening at the top of the neck.

Gerenuk are found only in small groups of three or four or possibly eight; or in pairs, or singly. They inhabit dry country with clumps or belts of matted, thorny bush, very often almost impenetrably dense. Here they browse off leaves and twigs, etc. They reach high into the thorny bushes with their long necks, but quite often, and very characteristically, stand right up on their hind legs, supporting their forelegs among the branches, to nibble the higher, succulent shoots or leaves.

The walk is curiously slouching and rather stiff—long neck held rigidly at a slight angle. When alarmed they trot or gallop nimbly in and out of the thorn bushes—their heads and necks held out straight before them. They are very inquisitive, and will stand perfectly still, staring at an unfamiliar object for some time. The comparatively open, dry country—dotted with thorny bushes and clumps—in the neighbourhood of Ol Tukai, at Amboseli, is ideal for viewing Gerenuk. Early mornings and late afternoons are the best times, however, as during the hotter hours they retire into the shade of the scrub.

GRANT'S GAZELLE

Gazella granti roosevelti (Heller)

(Kiswahili : *Swala granti*)

Field Impression.—The larger of the two common gazelles of Kenya. The rams are easily distinguished by their uniformly paler fawn colouring, larger area of white round buttocks, and large imposingly graceful, ringed horns, which extend upwards, outwards—slightly forwards and inwards at tips. Does have much smaller and more slender horns, and a more pronounced dark lateral stripe, than the rams.

Descriptive Notes.—The rams are pale sandy-rufous above, and white on the abdomen : the lateral stripe, so vivid in most of the gazelles, being indicated merely by a slightly darker tone along the flanks; or practically absent in some cases. The does have a much darker, almost black, lateral stripe : and may thereby be confused with

ROBERTSI

RAM ♂

EWE ♀

♂

♀

PETERSI

84

female Thomson's gazelle, unless the larger white area round buttocks, less black tail, larger size and longer horns are observed. Face white on sides, rufous on forehead and top of muzzle : with a dark band just above the nostrils, and dark round the eyes—extending in a narrow dark streak from eye to upper lip. The shining white of the rump is bordered by a dark margin, and the narrow tail is white with a black tuft. Female similar, except for much darker lateral stripe on flank, and smaller in size. Height of rams about 2 feet 6 inches at shoulder. Weight from about 150 to 165 lbs.

Horns.—In both sexes. Those of males are very long, massive at base, strongly ringed, curving very symmetrically upwards and backwards (sometimes slightly outwards in a lyrate manner) and finally inwards or forwards in a slight hook. The horns of *Granti* vary enormously, however, in curve; and on the Serengeti Plains of Tanganyika and in the Mara, a form *G. G. Robertsi* (Thomas) occurs in which the horns grow upwards, then widely outwards, finally downwards at the tips. *Female horns* are much more slender and shorter; curving slightly backwards and forwards at tips, ringed. Record horn length for a male is 30 inches. Average tip to tip interval 13 inches.

Distribution.—Very plentiful in Nairobi National Park : common in Amboseli National Reserve, and at Mara. It occurs in both eastern and western sections of Tsavo National Park, and is well represented at Marsabit, where three different subspecies (i.e. *Brighti, Notata,* and *Raineyi*) have been recorded. The Tsavo representatives are described as belonging to the subspecies *G.G. serengetae* (possibly also the Amboseli ones), in which the horns are said to diverge gradually, and are not lyrate in shape.

Habits.—In proportion to its body, the male Grant's gazelle has probably larger horns than any other African antelope. Its handsome colouring, and the proud bearing of the rams as they move about at a quick walk, holding their heads rather stiffly erect under the weight of their great horns, combine to make it always one of the most attractive of the East African antelopes. The horns of the does, though much shorter and more slender, are very gracefully curved. Grant's gazelle move about in troops of from five or six to thirty. The smaller lots usually consist of one big ram in

THOMSON'S GAZELLE
OR "TOMMY"

RAM ♂

EWES ♀ ♀

♀
TO SHOW
MALFORMATION
OF HORNS

"STOTTING"

86

charge of a number of ewes and younger males, and the big ram will always be noticed ambling along somewhat in the rear of the remainder of his troop. In longish grass only the tips of the bobbing horns are frequently visible.

Although dwelling largely in open plains' country, Grant's gazelle often frequent the more closely bushed acacia veld. They browse on leaves and shoots and eat grass. Blayney Percival records having found more Grant's gazelle killed by wild dogs than any other game.

THOMSON'S GAZELLE

Gazella thomsonii thomsonii (Gunther)

(Kiswahili : *Swala tomi*)

Field Impression.—This animal is very much smaller than Grant's gazelle, from which it can readily be distinguished when the two species are seen together by its vivid black lateral stripes and more reddish tone above. The dark brown stripe running from front corner of eye to upper lip is richer and more pronounced. Horns shorter and stouter and more upright, though gently backward curved. *Tail* black, and constantly wagged. Less white on rump than in Grant's. Female horns are very small and slender, often curiously twisted.

Descriptive Notes.—Thomson's gazelle is an attractive rich rufous-brown, becoming slightly paler along the flanks, and with a very clear-cut dark blackish-brown lateral stripe dividing the tawny-rufous of the upper flank and the white of the belly. The inner side of the rump is white, bordered by a thin dark line : but the white area is not nearly so extensive round the buttocks as it is in Grant's Gazelle. Centre of face rufous-brown with a black spot over the muzzle. A white line extends from above the eyes to the nostril, and below this a dark stripe runs from the eye to the upper lip. Tail short and narrow, black and tufted. Sexes are alike in colour. Height at shoulder about 2 feet. Weight of a ram 55-62 lbs.

Horns.—In both sexes. Those of males curve upwards and gently backwards with extreme tips slightly hooked forwards. They are closely ringed and nearly parallel. The female horns are very slender and nearly straight and very short. They are subject to the strangest errors of growth : sometimes one or other is twisted outwards or inwards, and sometimes the horns actually cross each other. Average length of male horns $14\frac{1}{2}$ inches. The Record is just under 17 inches.

Distribution.—The most plentiful and widely distributed of the smaller plains' game, but essentially a dweller in fairly open country. Very plentiful in Nairobi National Park, it is common also in Amboseli N.R. It is plentiful on the Keroghi Plateau, but does not occur in the Tsavo National Park.

Habits.—The Thomson's gazelle—or "Tommy"—may be seen almost everywhere throughout the open plains' game country, sometimes in very great numbers. From Grant's gazelle they can easily be distinguished by their smaller size and vivid black lateral stripes. The average party consists of a ram and several ewes; and the ram usually feeds slightly apart from, or behind, his little harem. As they move about, at a brisk walk, the little black tails are incessantly wagged and jerked—far more so than is the case with Grant's gazelle.

When alarmed, the "Tommy" often adopts that curious gait known as "stotting". He will suddenly begin a series of abrupt, bouncing jumps, with head and tail erect and all four legs stiffly straight : and ewes are said to do this when endeavouring to lure a jackal, or some other enemy, from the neighbourhood of the concealed young. In the open country at Amboseli, if one drives straight towards a solitary Tommy, he will often adopt this stotting manoeuvre for a few moments before finally making off.

Thomson's gazelle are naturally tame and confiding little creatures, quite often to be seen grazing among the Masai cattle; and a ram at Amboseli haunts the precincts of the Safari Lodge at Ol Tukai, which it frequently enters, enabling me to sketch it at close quarters.

Jackals prey on the newly-born Tommies—if they can find them unguarded, as the plucky little ram will not hesitate to chase the jackal away if he catches sight of it prowling nearby—and both leopard and cheetah, and wild dog, prey on the adults.

The young are born at the beginning of the rains in April and November, and I saw a very young fawn on June 17th (Ngorongoro Crater, Tanganyika). Usually only one fawn is born at a time, but twins have not infrequently been recorded. At first the mother leaves the herd and remains close to her infant, which will lie curled up on the ground, quite motionless, while she grazes nearby. Within a few hours the youngster is able to keep pace with its mother.

YELLOW-BACKED DUIKER

Cephalophus silvicultor silvicultor (Afzelius).

Field Impression.—A heavy, thickset animal as big as a goat; with short, backward-curved pointed horns and a tuft of rufous hairs on the crest between them. Blackish-brown, with yellow crest extending in the form of a triangle from withers to top of rump. Usually moves with head and short neck held low.

Descriptive Notes.—The following description is based on an excellent, and detailed one given by W. F. H. Ansell (*African Wild Life* Vol. 4. No. 2.) It is the largest of all the duikers, and entirely a dweller in dense forest. The colour, in both sexes, is a fairly uniform dark brown—almost blackish, a little darker along the back, and a little lighter on the lower limbs. Head, darkest between the eyes, has muzzle, cheeks and chin bluish white with a yellowish tinge. The crest between the horns varies between reddish and blackish : reddish in N. Rhodesian and East African specimens.

Extending from the withers to top of rump is a striking yellow dorsal marking which, broadening out as it does over the rump, forms a triangle. The rump patch is iron grey, being composed of mixed black and white hairs, and is more or less crescentic in shape, its front edge forming the base of the triangle. Ears rather short and rounded, with white inner margin. Tail short, with dark tuft at tip. The coat—

(MEDIUM)

(after BLANCOU)

on head, neck, and forequarters—is very short and close-lying, but on the back it lengthens, becoming longest at the base of the triangle. The rump patch hairs are short and close-lying in contrast. Shoulder height about 34 inches. Weight about 115 lbs.

Horns.—Present in both sexes, but thicker and longer in males. They project straight back, almost in a line with the head, with a slightly downward trend at the pointed tips, and are rather ruggedly ridged at the bases. Record length 7⅞ inches.

Distribution.—From Sierra Leone and the West African Forest region, east to the Mau forests of Kenya, and south to Angola and Northern Rhodesia. In the Mau forests of Kenya it has recently been discovered between Molo, Londiani and Kericho.

Habits.—Much has yet to be learned about the habits of this large forest duiker. It is rarely seen and is local in habit; only one pair usually inhabiting a certain area. It remains in the dense forest by day, only emerging into more open places by night. Very occasionally these creatures may be surprised in an open glade in the very early morning or very late evening. According to C. J. P. Ionides, they make nests under fallen trees or in very thick places where they lie up during the day; and the principal food consists of berries, leaves and bark of certain trees. It is said to carry its head low as it moves through the undergrowth, and can easily be mistaken for a Bush pig. It is usally found solitary—at most in pairs.

While we were resting, during a search for Mountain Gorilla on the slopes of Mount Mgahinga in Uganda, a curious "squealing" bark was heard, which our very experienced African guide assured us was made by a Yellow-backed Duiker.

Ionides records a newly born juvenile seen "in January and early February of 1946."

91

SMALL ANTELOPES

GREY BUSH DUIKER

Sylvicapra grimmia hindei (Wroughton)

(Kiswahili : *Nsya*)

Field Impression.—A small, fairly thickset grey-buff antelope, with a warm yellowish tinge, and a dark mark down
the centre of the face. There is a narrow tuft of hair
protruding between the horns, which are short and pointed
(in males only, normally) and set in almost a line with the
head. Fairly short tail, black above, white below. Runs
in a zigzag fashion, periodically taking a plunging leap.

Descriptive Notes.—The Bush Duiker is easily distinguished from most of the other small buck by its uniformly
greyish-buff tinge (a bit more yellow ochraceous in
East Africa than in the typical South African race, which is
greyer). The forehead is rufous, and a dark brown line
extends from the forehead to the top of the muzzle, and
is conspicuous in a front view. Ears rather narrow and
pointed and fairly long. Like all the duikers it has a
pronounced tuft or crest of long hairs projecting from the
top of the head between the horns, and this is present in
both sexes. The front of the forelegs is darker than the
rest of the body; and the tail is fairly short and narrow,
ending in a slight tuft : dark above, white underneath.
Shoulder height 23-25 inches. Weight up to about 35 lbs.
Females are usually slightly taller, and heavier, than males.
There are well-marked naked glandular lines below front
corners of eyes.

Horns.—In males only as a rule, though occasionally old
females grow rather stunted, thin horns. Fairly strongly
ridged at bases, they grow straight back in the line of the
head, inclining very slightly upwards, the tips quite straight
and pointed. They are set fairly close together. The
Kenya record horn length is less than 6 inches.

THE DUIKERS

(SMALL)

RAM

EWE ♀

GREY DUIKER ♂

HARVEY'S
RED DUIKER

BLUE
DUIKER

Distribution.—Although generally a commonly distributed small antelope in suitable country throughout Africa, the Grey Duiker is comparatively rare in Nairobi National Park, and this is also the case at Amboseli N.R., and in Mara N.R. It is recorded high up on Mount Kenya (this is a longer-haired, darker race of *Grimmia*—*s. g. Altivallis* Heller).

At Marsabit N.R. it is common, where it probably belongs to the race *s. g. Abyssinica* which is represented in the Tsavo National Park (East). It is fairly common in Tsavo N.P. (West).

Habits.—The common Bush Duiker is a solitary animal, dwelling in pairs as a rule, but often singly. In the Nairobi National Park, where it is not at all common (though occurring in many neighbouring localities), it is usually seen as a solitary example.

Duiker are both browsing and grazing animals, though on the whole they exist more generally on leaves, young shoots, beans and pods of Acacias, and berries and wild fruits of all sorts. Like Bushbuck, they are destructive to flower and vegetable produce in gardens or farms. They prefer more or less wooded country, and are never found in open, grassy plains. As duiker stroll about at ease, they constantly whisk their short tails : and, when alarmed, the tail is bobbed up and down, revealing the white under-surface, as they gallop away.

They are mostly nocturnal or crepuscular in habit, lying up by day in patches of grass or under shady bushes; however, in undisturbed areas, they may be seen by day, especially in dull weather. They are not so dependent on water as bushbuck. The rams are plucky little creatures which do not hesitate to charge or attack with their spiky horns when wounded or cornered, and sometimes become untrustworthy in captivity—though Duiker are easily tamed. When suspicious, they utter a curious "sniffy" sort of snort, and when snared, or caught by dogs, bleat most pitifully. The young are preyed on by Jackal and the smaller wild cats, eagles, etc., and the adults killed by wild dogs, leopards, Caracal and Serval, and Python.

The spoor is very narrow and pointed, and rather deeply set. Period of gestation about four months.

HARVEY'S RED DUIKER

Cephalophus harveyi harveyi (Thomas)

(Kiswahili : *Funo*)

Field Impression.—Thickset and short-necked, bright red-brown in colour with darker legs; slightly smaller than the Grey Duiker. Horns present in both sexes, very short, thick at base, and ridged there; extending backwards in line of head. Pronounced crest of long hair between the horns. Walks in a stealthy, almost crouching manner, with head and neck extended below line of back.

Descriptive Notes.—The Red Forest Duikers (*Cephalophus*)—of which the huge, previously-described, Yellow-backed Duiker is a member—differ, among other details, from the Bush Duikers (*Sylvicapra*) by the fact that the females also normally grow horns similar to, but slightly more slender, than those of the males. They are skulking creatures, dwelling in forest, long grass, or dense woodland, frequently in mountainous or hilly country; but like to sun themselves in open patches or on ridges.

Harvey's Red Duiker is the common one of Kenya (others extend all over suitable country in Africa from Natal north), and it is rich reddish-brown all over : darker on the centre line of the face and on the legs. Ears comparatively short and rounded. Tail about 4 inches long, tufted and insonspicuous. Height at shoulder 18-19 inches. Females larger and heavier than males. Weight 26-28 lbs. Tuft on head longer than in the Grey Duiker, nearly concealing the short triangular horns.

Horns.—In both sexes. Maximum length less than 5 inches. Very stout in the basal region and triangular in section, they are heavily ringed at base, and slope backwards in the line of the face, and are set close together.

Distribution.—Harvey's Red Duiker is common in Nairobi National Park, Amboseli N.R., and in Mara N.R. In Tsavo National Park (West) it is frequently seen on Mungai, and it is also seen in the Eastern section of Tsavo. It is recorded from Marsabit National Reserve.

Habits.—Harvey's Red Duiker dwell usually in pairs,

or as solitary individuals, in thick covert of some sort : wooded banks of streams or rivers, lush hillsides with rank undergrowth, and the forested or wooded gullies of mountains. They are among the most difficult antelope of which to obtain a good view—not only owing to the dense nature of their usual environment, but also because they are largely nocturnal : lying up in long grass or thickets during the day, and feeding at night, early mornings or late afternoons. They seem to be entirely browsers, partaking of leaves, shoots, berries, bean-pods, etc., though possibly certain grasses may be grazed occasionally. Contrary to the case with the common Grey Duiker, water, in regular supply, is an absolute necessity to the Red Duiker. They are attractive little fellows, with their foxy-red coats, and it is a pity that one's usual contact with them is merely the sound of a scurrying rush, varied with the usual bounding jumps, through the dense under-growth.

According to Colonel Stevenson-Hamilton, both Grey and Red Duiker probably have no set breeding season. He describes the cry, or alarm note, as a "compromise between a whistle and a sniff." A sound which I heard on the wooded slopes of Mount Mgahinga, in Uganda, and which was stated by the guide to be the call of a Red Duiker, might well have been described thus.

BLUE DUIKER

Cephalophus monticola musculoides (Heller)

(Kiswahili : *Paa*)

Field Impression.—A minute antelope—hardly larger than a hare. Greyish-brown ("mousy"), rather more rufous-tinged along back and legs. Middle-line of ventral surface, throat, chin and underparts of legs white. Horns (males only) very small and short. Inhabits only dense forest or woodland country, never seen in the open.

Descriptive Notes.—The Blue Forest Duikers (*Guevei*) represent the third group of the Duikers, and are the smallest members of the Group: dwelling always in forested or thickly wooded areas—especially in the Coastal areas, from the Cape northwards. The Southern African species differ from their East African relatives in that horns are present in both sexes in the former, and only in the males in the latter. The females are usually larger and slightly heavier than the males. They are all more or less greyish-brown, browner above and greyer on flanks, with rufous-tinged legs, and more or less white underparts. Shoulder height about 13 inches.

Horns.—In the Kenya Race only present in the males, normally. They are set in a slight angle to the plane of the face, and are extremely small, ringed at base, and rarely exceed 2 inches in length. The Record is 2½ inches. Spread 1¾ inches.

Distribution.—So far, apparently, only recorded from Mara National Reserve, though it may well yet be found in suitable localities in some of the National Parks and Reserves.

Habits.—I have no personal experience at all of this most attractive little creature, so must draw on the records of others. A. H. Garnet Blamey (South Africa) remarks that its rotund body appears rather heavy when compared with its slender legs and tiny hooves, and that its skin is of an extremely tensile toughness: strips of it being usable for sewing with a needle, and "can make excellent boot-laces"! Although normally a dweller in very dense places, the same authority states that *Piti* (Zulu) frequently emerge on to the open beaches bordering dune-forests in Natal, and even swim out to sea when hunted. It feeds on a variety of leaves, shoots, and stinging-nettles of the forest, and greedily devours wild figs and other delicacies extravagantly dropped and scattered by feeding monkeys. After veld fires, it will come out to feed on tender young grass sprouting from the burnt areas, but is intensely alert, and quick to dive back to cover at the first alarm.

Like all duikers, the Blue Duiker has a jerky, zigzag gait as it darts through the bush, and being so small it can move freely *below* the level of the undergrowth. The ears are very short and rounded at tips. The short, hairy tail—

brown above and white below—would be invisible except that its constant flicking, as the little creature moves about, exposes the white in tiny flashes.

Unfortunately these little forest duikers leave well-marked trails or paths, so that the native snarer finds them an easy prey. A snared, or otherwise caught, Blue Duiker, "gives utterance to pitiful, loud, strangely cat-like miaulings." "Their small cleft hoof-prints are too small for one's fingertips to fit." The Great Crowned Eagle (*Stephanoetus coronatus*) preys on adults and young blue duiker : and Python, wild cats of various sorts, leopards, and so on, in addition to man and his dogs and snares, complete the tally of enemies.

KENYA ORIBI

Ourebia ourebi cottoni (Thomas)

(Kiswahili : *Taya*)

Field Impression.—A neatly built, bright rufous-fawn antelope with short, but conspicuously black-tipped, tail : rather larger and taller than a steenbok, which it somewhat resembles, though with shorter and less broad ears. At fairly close quarters, or through glasses, a naked circular spot below the ear can be seen as a dark spot. Horns, in rams only, fairly short, pointed, and straight up from the head. Usually seen in pairs, or small parties of three or four.

Descriptive Notes.—The Oribi, which occurs in a number of local races from the Cape throughout Africa as far as 13° north lat., is the largest of the *Neotragine* group of small antelopes (which includes the Steenbok, Grysbok, Sunis and Pygmy antelopes). It has a well-marked bare glandular patch or spot beneath each ear, and curious tufts of hair developed on the knees (these are not really visible in the field), while the strikingly black brushy tip to the short tail is a very helpful field character. Lateral hooves are present. The colour is a rich golden-fawn, more

(SMALL)

ORIBI

♂

RAM

"STOTTING"
GAIT

99

rufous on back, and white below. The tail in the East African form is said to be shorter, and not quite so black above, as in the Cape Oribi (Lydekker). Shoulder height from 22-24 inches. Weight up to 40 lbs. Ears narrow and pointed, fairly long but not so proportionately large as in the Steenbok. There is a black patch on the forehead between the horns, and large black glandular spots in front of the eyes.

Horns.—In males only. Slender and pointed, more or less ringed about half-way up, growing erect from above the orbits with a slight forward tendency at the smooth and pointed tips. Maximum recorded length 5¾ inches (Kenya Race).

Distribution.—In the present National Parks and National Reserves of Kenya the Oribi has been but scantily recorded. There have been two reports of a single Oribi in Nairobi National Park, and it is reported as common in Mara N.R. There are so far no records from either Tsavo (East or West), Marsabit, or the Mountain National Parks.

Habits.—Oribi seem to be rather catholic in taste, inhabiting open downs and elevations up to 8,000 feet, where they lie in grassy hollows, or sheltered slopes, or among outcropping rocks on the higher levels : while in the lower country they occur among palm-groves, or in low, scrubby bush. They are found in pairs, or groups of three or four to half a dozen, and are at once recognisable from Steenbok (which they resemble rather in colour, though more gold-hued above) by their taller build and rather shorter ears. When alarmed, they start off at a brisk gallop, then begin a curious "stotting" action: springing into the air with all four legs held straight and stiff, after every few bounds. The black tail is usually wagged vigorously during the manoeuvre. When going at full pace, Oribi can move with great speed, and then gallop with head and neck stretched out in front.

P. Trewhela has noted, in Natal, that the Oribi "when disturbed never seems to run in a straight line for its objective, but always along a curved route. Perhaps this is because it prefers to follow the contours of the land . . . On a hot afternoon, Oribi frequently rest in a donga or hollow, where the grass is fairly long and dense, and where they can receive the full warmth of the sun while protected frcm the wind. At this time they are particularly hard to see, as only the head—so like a rock from a distance—protrudes above the grass. They will lie in this position, hardly flicking an ear, until the day is cooler (at sunset) when they rise again and resume feeding." An inquisitive oribi, approaching the observer and his companion who were sitting motionless on an open hill, came forward a few yards, stared hard, and then uttering a squeak, jumped back a few paces—to continue the performance until, her suspicions confirmed, she bounded away. Pitman describes this alarm call as a shrill whistle. The droppings (each about $\frac{1}{4}$ inch long) are deposited in regularly resorted to "middens." The Oribi is essentially a grazer and is never found far from water. The fawns are born in the dry season, before the rains (Pitman).

STEENBOK

Raphicerus campestris neumanni (Matschie)

(Kiswahili : Tondoro)

Field Impression.—A Small, very graceful rufous-fawn coloured antelope rather smaller than a Grey Duiker. It is pure white on the adomen and inside the legs, and has white eyebrows; and its tail is a mere tuft hardly visible. The ears are very large and oval, and the horns (males only) project straight up over the orbits with a very slight forward curve at extreme tips.

Descriptive Notes.—The Steinbuck, or Steenbok, is one of the most graceful and widely distributed of the small antelopes. Its rich rufous-fawn colouring at once distinguishes it from the common duiker, but in colour it more resembles the larger Oribi. From this its far larger ears and shorter head in proportion, and absence of any black on the tail, and also that it occurs only singly or in pairs, should distinguish it. There is usually a small black

(SMALL)

STEENBOK

RAM

EWE

KLIPSPRINGER

mark just above the nose, and a dark cresentic mark on the crown between the horns—but these features are not always constant. The Steenbok has no lateral, or "false" hooves. There are large, conspicuous black glandular orifices in front of the eyes. Shoulder height about 22 inches. Weight 25-33 lbs.

Females usually larger than males.

Horns.—Males only. Set very widely in the head and projecting immediately above the orbits, from which they grow almost vertically but with a slight, gentle forward curve at the tips. They are smooth and very narrow and sharp. Whereas in the common Duiker the horns are in the same plane of the face : in the Steenbok they grow almost at right angles. Record horn length in Kenya is under 6 inches. Two records from the Cape measured $7\frac{1}{2}$ inches and $7\frac{3}{8}$ inches respectively.

Distribution.—The Steenbok is common in Nairobi National Park, Tsavo N.P. (East and West), Amboseli, and Marsabit. It is not yet recorded from Mara.

Habits.—Almost entirely a grazing antelope, the Steenbok is an inhabitant of grassy plains and fairly lightly bushed savanna country, but never in thickly wooded or forest areas. It is usually seen singly, or in pairs, and at first sight of supposed danger usually squats in the grass, watching the intruder. If it is really alarmed, it will then spring up and dart away in a rather zigzag direction, varying its frisky little gallop with a few jumps now and then. It seldom goes very far before halting to glance back, when, if its fears are allayed, it will take a few trotting steps, with whisking tufty tail, before settling down to graze, or rest, as it feels inclined. When hunted by dogs (wild or native), cheetah, etc., Steenbok frequently run to ground in any handy deserted antbear burrow or other hole. The larger eagles, Caracel and Serval, and Python, all prey on Steenbok when opportunity offers, but perhaps their two most deadly foes are the African Wild Hunting Dogs and the Cheetah. The young are pounced on by jackal and hyena. In spite of this formidable array of enemies (not to mention man and his snares and dogs), the Steenbok manages to survive and continues to be fairly well dis-tributed all over Africa south of the Sahara—even in fairly closely settled areas.

SUNI, OR PIGMY ANTELOPE

Nesotragus moschatus akeleyi (Heller)

(Kiswahili : *Paa*)

Field Impression.—The very smallest of the East African Antelopes, even smaller than the Dik-Dik, or Blue Duiker. More brown than grey, with white belly and rather large ears. No forehead tuft, and tiny horns are more conspicuous than in the Dik-Dik; strongly ridged, and project from the head backwards and slightly upwards at tips.

Descriptive Notes.—The Sunis are near relativ s of the Oribis, from which they are distinguished by absence of naked patch below the ear, and lack of lateral hooves. The general colour of this Kenya species is grizzled fawn-grey, with a rufous tinge. There is a white area on the throat, divided by a median darker band, and the belly is white. Tail, a mere tuft, the same colour at back. The deep, linear face-glands (in front of the eyes) exhale a strong odour of musk, which causes these animals sometimes to be alluded to as "Musk Antelopes" (not to be confused with the Musk Deer). Shoulder height 13-14 inches.

Horns.—in males only. Set wide apart, they project backwards in a line with the face and then curve slightly upwards at pointed tips. Strongly ridged, nearly as far as the tips. The record length is under 3½ inches.

Distribution.—The Suni is rare in Nairobi National Park, but occurs there. It is reported as being common in the Western section of Tsavo National Park, but has so far not been recorded from Amboseli, Mara, or Marsabit National Reserves.

Habits.—The Suni is mainly a dweller in forest-patches or bushy thickets, and is seldom seen in the open country. Glimpses, however, may occasionally be caught of one in an open glade, especially in early mornings or late afternoons—as they appear to be largely nocturnal feeders. They eat leaves, shoots, berries, etc., and grass. When disturbed, they dart away, twisting and turning about the

SUNI

(SMALL)

KIRK'S DIK-DIK

trees and bushes and are soon lost to sight. They are said to utter a short, barking cry (a much reduced edition of that of the Bushbuck) and a sharp whistling snort.

KIRK'S DIK-DIK

Rhynchotragus kirkii hindei (Thomas)

GUENTHER'S DIK-DIK

Rhynchotragus guentheri smithii (Thomas)

(Kiswahili : *Dikidiki*)

Field Impression.—Exceedingly small antelopes, standing only about 15 inches, or less, at the shoulder. The nose is rather elongated, in a proboscis-like manner, and the horns very short, half concealed in a tuft of hair (broader than the duikers). More or less drab-grey in colouring with paler circles round the eyes. Conspicuous black glandular patches in front of the eyes. Horns only in males. Usually seen in couples, or singly.

Descriptive Notes.—Kirk's Dik-Dik is the common one of Kenya—Guenther's occurring only in the northern area. They are much alike in general appearance, though Guenther's has a more conspicuously elongated proboscis, is larger in size, and is more uniformly greyish-drab in colour : whereas Kirk's Dik-Dik has markedly reddish-fulvous limbs, and is more yellowish-tinged on the flanks. The tail, in both species, is so short as to be almost rudimentary, and minute lateral hooves are present. The elongated, slightly downward curved muzzle is almost entirely covered with hair, and there is a well-marked crest or tuft on the forehead. The females are slightly larger than the males. Weight : 8¼ lbs (Guenther). Shoulder-height : 14-16 inches.

Horns.—Present only in males. Exceedingly short, projecting back in the plane of the head, slightly curving upwards at the pointed tips; with strong basal ribs. They are hardly visible among the head tuft. In Kirk's, the record is less than 4 inches, about 2¾ inches being the average. In Guenther's, the horns measure from about 3 inches to 3⅜ inches.

Distribution.—Kirk's Dik-Dik is common in Nairobi National Park, Tsavo N.P. (East and West), Amboseli and Mara National Reserves. Guenther's Dik-Dik is the type inhabiting Marsabit National Reserve.

Habits.—The Dik-Diks are plentiful everywhere in the scrubby bush or "niyika," and may easily be noticed, either standing gazing inquisitively at a passing car or departing rapidly in a series of frisky little hops and bounds through the tussocky herbage. They are fascinating little creatures —hardly larger than hares—and are generally seen in pairs, or singly—though very occasionally parties of five or six are noticed. They appear to be largely crepuscular, or nocturnal in habit, mostly lying up under bushes or tufts of grass during the day (at any rate during the hotter hours). They are also said to be almost independent of water, and are found in the driest places. The minute droppings are deposited regularly in one place—very frequently over the droppings of rhino, according to Swayne in Somaliland. The young are very carefully concealed, and hardly ever seen; and Dik-dik are notorious for their fidelity to a certain chosen neighbourhood.

KLIPSPRINGER

Oreotragus oreotragus schillingsi (Neumann)

(Kiswahili : *Mbuzi mawe*)

Field Impression.—A small, thickset, rather rough-coated antelope always found either on, or within the near neighbourhood of rocky outcrops or escarpments. Uniform olive-brown, with a yellowish tinge, and white below and on throat. Horns short, ringed and upright over eyes— present in both sexes. It stands on the very tips of its curious, narrow, almost cylindrical-shaped hooves. Tail short.

Descriptive Notes.—Slightly larger than the Steenbok, and very much more stocky and thickly-set in form, the most curious feature about the Klipspringer is its coarse, pithy coat (unlike that of any other antelope, the hairs being comparable to those of the Asiatic Musk deer)—formerly much used by pioneers and hunters in South Africa for stuffing their saddles! In colour the hairs are olive-grey, tipped with yellow—imparting a characteristically speckled look to the coat as a whole. In the race inhabiting Kenya, the coat is not so uniform above as in South Africa, being darker along the back, and clear grey, or rufous, along the thighs. The ears are large, as in the steenbok, usually shaggily fringed at the tips. The pit-like glandular orifices in front of the eyes are very large and conspicuous, and the tail is short and rather stumpy. The hooves are set in a peculiar way specially adapted for clinging to and balancing on small projections of rock. They are narrow and cylindrical, and only the tips rest on the ground. There are also well-developed lateral hooves. Shoulder height (rams), 20-22 inches. Weight : 35-40 lbs. (approx.).

Horns.—In the Kenya race present in both sexes (only in males as a rule in South Africa). Short and spiky, rising almost vertically above the eyes with a slight forward curvature, basal third ringed. East African record is 5 inches.

Distribution.—Rare in Nairobi National Park, and may occur on Ol Doinyo Orok at Amboseli. It is common in Mara N.R., and in the Marsabit N.R. It is frequently seen on Mungai, in Tsavo N.P. (West), and also occurs in Eastern Tsavo. It does not occur in the Mountain National Parks.

Habits.—Klipspringer must always be looked for when passing rocky hillocks (koppies) or stony hillsides, etc. They may frequently be observed perched high up on ledges, poised gracefully with all four feet close together on a ledge; or perhaps nimbly racing up a cliff or rock face with the agility of a chamois. More often they will be seen feeding quietly in the vegetation growing within a short distance of the base of such rock formations—to which they will always repair when alarmed. They must be looked for carefully, as their olive "pepper and salt" colouring, and small forms are easily overlooked among the scrub that usually grows round the base of such hills. Also, when passing koppies, few people think of scanning the rocks themselves!

Klipspringers utter a curious little abrupt snort—which sounds very like a child's penny trumpet out of a cracker. They are delightful, smug-looking little creatures, and though always very alert, are very inquisitive. The hindquarters are particularly powerful and rounded, enabling them to bound and jump with ease up the steepest gradients. Their principal food consists of small shrubs and grasses growing at the foot of stony outcrops, etc., and they appear to be almost independent of water—probably getting sufficient moisture from the dew, or hollows in rocks. Leopards and the larger wild cats, pythons, and the larger eagles and hawks are their principal enemies the latter mainly taking the young when opportunity serves. A single kid is born during the rainy season, or just before it.

THE GIRAFFES

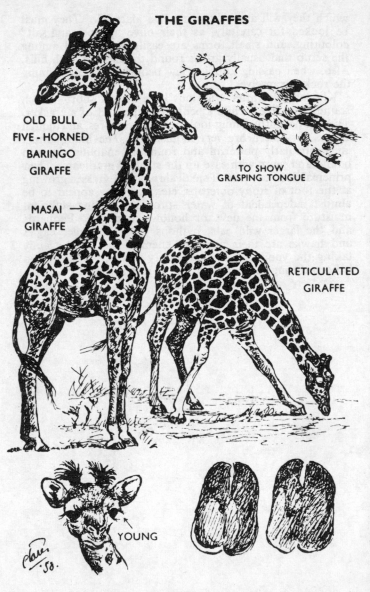

OLD BULL
FIVE - HORNED
BARINGO
GIRAFFE

TO SHOW
GRASPING TONGUE

MASAI →
GIRAFFE

RETICULATED
GIRAFFE

YOUNG

THE GIRAFFES

1. RETICULATED GIRAFFE

Giraffa reticulata (De Winton)

(Kiswahili : *Twiga*)

Field Impression.—A rich liver-red animal, marked with a coarse *network* of narrow white lines, decreasing in size towards the head but everywhere large. The liver markings on body and lower neck are mostly quadrangular (though somewhat irregular in size), and are distinct from the blotchy, or rounded, markings on the common species of Giraffe. Lower parts of the legs more or less whitish.

2. MASAI GIRAFFE

Giraffa camelopardalis tippelskirchi (Matschie)

(Kiswahili : *Twiga*)

Field Impression.—Ground colour more or less buff, marked with irregularly-shaped, usually rather jagged-edged, often star-like markings of irregular size : varying from very dark brown to darker or paler chestnut in colour. Forehead and front of face usually greyish. Area round eyes and front of cheeks whitish. Usually well spotted below the eyes. Muzzle more or less rufous, as is the short, hogged mane down back of neck. Legs more or less spotted below the knees (particularly the hind legs) on a tan ground, becoming white just above the hooves.

Tail, in both species : long with a long brush of black hairs at tip. Upper lip broad and rather protrusive, nostrils slit-like and covered with hair. *Height* up to fifteen feet at top of horns in females, and up to eighteen feet, or a little over, in males. *Shoulder height:* about 12 feet in bulls; 8-9½ feet in cows. *Weight* about a ton (bull).

Horns.—These, of course, are not truly horns in Giraffe, but simply projections of bone, covered (except at the tips in adults) with skin and hair. They are said to be the remains of cores which, in extinct ancestral forms supported a form of antler similar to those in modern deer. In the adult bulls they grow massive and fairly tall (up to about nine inches from top of skull), in cows they are shorter and less massive.

In calves, the "horns" are first indicated by tassel-like tufts of hair. In addition to the main horns, a prominent outgrowth of bone projects from the forehead between the eyes, and in old bulls of both species frequently becomes sufficiently massive almost to resemble a third horn (in the Baringo, or Rothschild's race of *Camelopardalis* from Uganda and western Kenya, and in *Cottoni* which seems to be only a variation of the former, this central horn is often so pronounced in old bulls as to warrant the name "Five-horned" Giraffe!) In this connection, behind the main horns, adult bulls of both races develop curious bony knobs at the base of the skull, which can be said to resemble a second pair of horns (though short ones).

The colouration of *Tippelskirchi*, and the actual form of the markings, vary considerably : some having the typical, jagged markings—others having a more rounded, blotched pattern (as may be noticed any day in Nairobi National Park), and the latter are usually darker coloured animals, so whether the Baringo and Masai Giraffes interlink remains to be settled. This same individual variation, as in the case of the Burchill's zebras, can be noticed all over Africa—but *Reticulata* is a distinct species, very locally distributed.

Distribution.—The Marsabit National Reserve is theonly park containing the *Reticulated Giraffe*, which is the sole species occurring in that area. *The Masai Giraffe* is common in Nairobi National Park, Tsavo N.P. (East and West), Amboseli N.R., and at Mata N.R. Giraffes, of course, do not exist in the Mountain National Parks.

Habits.—Giraffe, of course, are browsing animals, specialised to enable them to reach high among the foliage of the thorny acacias which form their favourite food. When at close quarters, it is interesting to observe the long, narrow grey tongues with which the foliage, or shoots, are grasped. When drinking the head can be sufficiently lowered only by the widespread straddling of the long limbs, which result in a most ungainly, awkward attitude. In spite of the length of the neck, it contains only the same number of vertebrae (seven) as in the human neck! Giraffes are extraordinarily gentle creatures, which rarely make any attempt at aggressive attack, even when wounded. None-the-less, in such circumstances or when attacked by lions (or when a cow wishes to defend her calf), they kick powerfully with their immense hooves, and "chop" with the forelimbs, and such blows would have almost the power of sledge hammers, and many an attacking lion must have been thus crumpled up   Bulls fight by pounding away at each other's necks and shoulders with their massive heads : but such fights seem curiously lacking in violent emotion, though the Giraffe may continue wearily circling round and round each other for quite lengthy periods, and a shrewd blow could easily break a neck. Originally believed to be voiceless, it is now generally agreed that the giraffe occasionally utters a curious, subdued, husky sort of grunt, and the writer has distinctly heard this on more than one occasion. An alarmed animal will snort, before "galumphing" away in its curious "slow-motion" gallop wherein the hind limbs come well before the fore limbs, and the tail is slowly waved from side to side, or curled up in a loop over the rump. The walking gait is like that of the camel—both limbs on the same side moving forward together. Lions are the only natural enemies of adults, though leopards have been known to attack the young (Selous), and in such an attack a giraffe will gallop fast through the thickest bush he can find, often thereby dislodging his less thick-skinned opponent. It is likely that lions will only attack them when they are found in the open, and probably it is a concerted attack as a rule. Contrary to popular belief, giraffe quite often lie down in the grass, though they usually keep their long necks up. They will doze with

Give them the feeling of the country you're in

You're best expressed on a Photolette

114

heads resting in the crotch of a tree. Old bulls exude a very unpleasant, powerful stench.

The enormous hoof prints are unmistakable; in big bulls they may measure twelve inches in length. The droppings are large pellets with one end flattened. Giraffe have very acute sight, and their great eyes dark, heavily lashed, are among the most beautiful of all animals, the heavy lids imparting a rather melancholy expression.

EAST AFRICAN HIPPOPOTAMUS

Hippopotamus amphibius kiboko (Heller)

(Kiswahili : *Kiboko*)

Descriptive Notes.—General appearance familiar and needs no description. The short legs are provided with four toes encased in rounded hooves, all of which touch the ground when walking. In the enormous head with its broad and sqaure muzzle, notable features are the slit-like nostrils which can be closed under water, the short, rounded ears, and the prominent "periscope" eyes; formed, like those of frog and crocodile, to enable observation just above the surface. Notable also is the short, laterally compressed tail—its tip decorated with a few sparse bristles. The colour of adults ranges from almost black to dark brown, with an admixture of fleshy pink round sides of face and underparts. Young animals are generally paler than adults. The bulls are much larger, and heavier, with longer tusks, than the cows. *Mammae*, 2. *Shoulder height* up to 4 feet 10 inches or so (bulls) and about 4 feet 6 inches (cows). *Length* (from snout to tail) about 14 feet (bull). *Weight* of bulls up to 4 tons, and occasionally possibly even 5 tons.

Tusks.—Four large, curved tusks, with flattened shear-like edges, project from the front corners of each jaw, and between them in the lower jaw the large incisors project almost straight forwards; in the upper jaw the direction is downwards. Rowland Ward records the longest, not malformed, tusk, as 41½ inches; and the longest straight tusk as 23⅜ inches. A good average curved tusk will measure 30 inches, and a good straight one 20 inches (Lyell). Hippo ivory, being softer than that of elephant, is used very largely in the production of ivory curios, etc., it has no visible grain.

Distribution.—The Hippo can easily be seen in the Athi River in Nairobi National Park, where about half-a-dozen

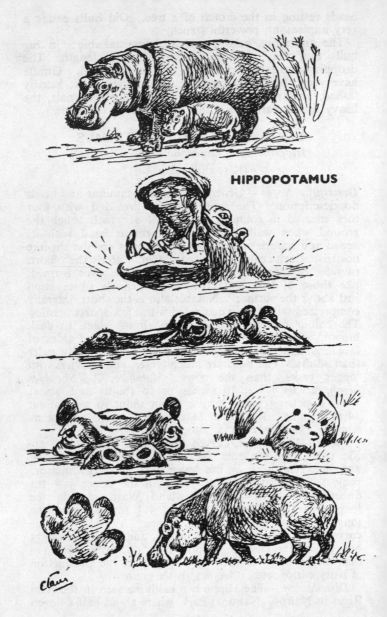

HIPPOPOTAMUS

are at present estimated to reside. It occurs in the swamp at Amboseli, and is common in Mara N.R. Mzima Springs in western Tsavo Park, is the most fascinating place to observe Hippo. The crystal-clear water enables one to observe their method of walking under water from the raised platform provided there, and, if one is fortunate, hippo (and crocodiles) may be watched disporting among the numerous fishes from the under water glass-fronted "observation tank." They are plentiful in Eastern Tsavo as well. In Marsabit N.R. a school of about 25-30 Hippo are to be found in the Uaso Nyiro river near the S.W. corner of the Reserve; a few may generally be seen in the pools of the Upper Seya, and a few also live near the El Molo tribe in Lake Rudolph.

Habits.—The aptness of the ancient Greek name of "River Horse" can be observed when looking at the upper part of a hippo's head as it appears above the water. When completely submerged, hippo have still to raise every 3—5 minutes at any rate, their nostrils, above the surface in order to breathe. Where much persecuted, they will project only the nostrils, and those under overhanging reeds or other covert. Normally, they raise the whole head blowing the water noisily from the nostrils, and vigorously wagging their small ears. At such times an inquisitive hippo may utter his deep, rumbling : "*Hoosh! HAW-haw-haw-haw*," at which frequently the rest of the herd may join in concert. As a rule they emerge from the water to graze along the riverside vegetation only at night : spending the day submerged, or dozing in heaps, one head upon another, on rocks or sandbars : but in certain areas (such as the Queen Elizabeth Park of Uganda) they prowl about overland and graze all day.

Although so good-natured in aspect, and quiveringly obese in form, male hippos are most violent and courageous fighters, and inflict fearful wounds on one another with sideways slashes of the great shear-like canines. Quite often such fights end in the death of one or the other. Occasional old bulls become truculent, and attack water-craft passing in their domain, while to get between a hippo on land and the water is a most dangerous proceeding. Generally speaking, though, the hippo is an inoffensive beast, provided he is left alone. The small calf is at first left concealed in the herbage adjacent to the water, but at an early age climbs on to the mother's back when she enters the water.

The principal natural function of the hippo is to keep down the aquatic vegetation bordering streams and rivers and particularly, by creating paths and channels through dense floating masses of papyrus and "sudd," to enable the water to flow and thereby prevent blockages. Where hippo have been artificially reduced in such habitats, the effects have been most deleterious.

The droppings, which are somewhat of the consistency of, though smaller than those of elephant, are scattered about by vigorous tail wagging, and, when deposited on land, are recognisable by the way in which they are splashed about over the herbage. The enormous four-toed tracks are easily recognisable and are made in parallel lines. Mating takes place in the water, the cow usually more or less submerged. Although they escape the attentions of the ticks which irritate most entirely land-dwelling animals in Africa, hippos are much pestered by leeches in the water. They are often inclined to attack camp-fires burning too close to their favourite pools at night. On the whole, hippo and crocodiles take little notice of one another, and bask on the same rocks, but a mother hippo will drive all crocs away from the neighbourhood of her young one. The intensely thick skin was originally in great demand for those terrible whips known as "sjamboks" in South Africa, and "Kibokos" in East Africa.

THE AFRICAN WILD PIGS

1. GIANT FOREST HOG

Hylochoerus meinertzhageni meinertzhageni (Thomas)

(Kiswahili : *Nguruwe ?*)

Field Impression.—An enormous, heavily built, hairy, black pig, found only in forests or the immediate vicinity of them. Boars have huge warty excrescences below the eyes; tusk shaped like, though smaller than, those of warthog. Coat jet-black without markings of any sort. General attitude much like that of a giant Bush Pig.

Descriptive Notes.—The Forest Hog in many ways has points resembling both Bush Pig and Warthog. The form of its short, untufted ears, the very wide snout, the shape of the tusks, and the enormous semicircular warty growths on the cheeks—all these recall the warthog. On the other hand the shaggy coat, covered with long black bristles, bulky form, and habits generally, are more reminiscent of the Bush Pig. General colouration black, but the fungus-like growths below the eyes are more or less flesh-coloured. Snout and muzzle exceedingly broad. The boars are larger, with longer tusks and more massive facial "warts," than the sows. I have seen no description of the young. Shoulder height up to about 32 inches. A large boar from French Equatorial Africa weighed clean 299½ lbs., but the Kenya examples are said to grow heavier than those of West Africa.

Tusks.—Upper ones widespread, curving upwards at tips. The lower tusks are almost, but not quite, as long as the upper ones : grinding against them with a flattened, razor-sharp edge. Largest recorded total length of upper tusk (Kenya) is 12¼ inches, with a circumference of 4⅝ inches. Largest total length of a lower tusk (Kenya) is 9⅞ inches (circumference 2⅝ inches).

GIANT FOREST HOG

Distribution.—The Giant Forest Hog is the most locally distributed of the African pigs, and was only discovered in 1904 when Colonel R. Meinertzhagen sent portions of the skin, and a skull, to the British Museum (Natural History). These original specimens were obtained on Mount Kenya, and from the Nandi forest. It occurs in the Mau forest and the Elgon District. Owing to its strictly forest habitat, it is rarely seen, but has been recorded as fairly common in Mara National Reserve. It is common in the Aberdares National Park, and may quite often be seen drinking at "Treetops" (a trip to the latter is worth while for this opportunity alone). It does not occur in either Nairobi N.P., Tsavo N.P., or in Amboseli N.R. In Marsabit it is at present known to occur only in the forests on Karisia, where it is not plentiful.

Habits.—Having never yet seen a Giant Forest Hog, I cannot give any personal impressions of its aspect in its habitat, but the black mass of its bulk, half-concealed among undergrowth in the gloom of the forest, is said to resemble that of a small rhino or buffalo. I have seen tunnels through the undergrowth said to have been made by them, and these are very similar to, though rather larger, than those of Bush Pig, and like them are usually lined with the droppings. Like the Bongo, it remains faithful to certain localities.

Habits, generally, seem to be very similar to those of Bush Pig, though I think they are found more often in pairs, or family groups, and not in such large sounders. Both in East and West Africa this huge pig has the reputation for ferocity when attacked or unduly disturbed, and it is stated (Powell-Cotton) that "if the male sees a sow wounded, or is hit himself, he can be counted upon to make a determined attack, and once he succeeds in knocking a man down, not even a cutlass will induce him to leave his victim."

"When the female is about to farrow, she and the male cut down a quantity of grass to prepare a large bed, into which she creeps while he continues to pile it over her. It is easy for hunters to find these beds and shoot the female, but they know they will have to reckon with an enraged male who guards the spot with vigilance. He is held in even greater respect than Buffalo by the natives."

BUSH PIG

When alarmed, Forest Hog stampede loudly through the undergrowth with a succession of deep grunts and snorts—like Bush Pig.

2. KENYA BUSH PIG

Potamochoerus porcus keniae (Lönnberg)

(Kiswahili : *Nguruwe*)

Field Impression.—Rarely seen by day as very nocturnal, and a dweller in dense, bushy or grassy undergrowth—along margins of streams or rivers and forested or wooded ravines in hilly country. It is covered with a wiry coat of long reddish-brown bristles, with white along back ridge, greyish-white face and blackish cheeks and legs. Ears tipped with pencilled tufts of long hair; face long and pointed with protruding knobs below eyes; tusks short and knife-like; carries its tail hanging down when trotting.

Descriptive Notes.—The Bush Pig varies a great deal in colour : some specimens being almost black, or dark brown —others reddish or reddish-brown above (younger ones are invariably more bright, foxy-reddish than older specimens)—but all agree in having a dorsal crest of long, erectile white and black bristles, and most of the upper part of the face is white, or greyish white, with dark patches round the eyes, and blackish cheeks. Underparts, and limbs, are blackish as well. The ears are pointed, and bear at their tips long, pencilled tufts of hairs. There is a swollen area below the eyes, and in front of them, on the upper sides of the muzzle, two projecting "nobs" (one on either side) which are mere protuberances in the sows. As in all pigs, the lateral hooves are large.

The newly-born young are dark brown with horizontally extended yellow stripes—like the young of Wild Boar. A large male weighs about 170 lbs. or more with a shoulder height of about 31 inches.

Tusks.—Short, stout, and very sharp : the top ones forming a blunt, flat-edged "hone" against which the knife-like lower tusks are perpetually sharpened. Average length of lower tusks 6-7 inches.

Distribution.—Bush Pig are only found in fairly dense covert. They are common in suitable areas of Nairobi National Park, and Mara N.R., but so far have not been recorded at Amboseli. They are common, though not often seen, in Tsavo N.P. (East and West); and they occur in the Marsabit area. They are almost certain to be plentiful in the Mountain National Parks.

Habits.—Even where plentiful, Bush Pig are rarely seen by day except during wet or cloudy weather when they remain on the move longer, and may feed throughout the day. Normally, they are strictly nocturnal, leaving their daytime retreats under thickets, in long grass, dense bush or reedbeds, etc., at dusk, or shortly after, and often travelling some miles to their chosen feeding grounds (particularly if these be among cultivated crops). By dawn they are usually back in covert again. They travel in sounders of from five to six animals to as many as twenty or more, a large "master" boar usually ruling the sounder and maintaining a vigorous discipline. They are omnivorous, like all pigs, devouring grass, roots, seeds and wild fruits; insects, snakes and other reptiles when encountered; birds' eggs, the rhizomes of various forest ferns, and carrion of any age or quality! Antelopes in snares have been killed and devoured by them. To all cultivated crops they are fearfully destructive, trampling and rending as much as they devour.

The boars are courageous and truculent in the extreme, and will often charge dogs merely on sight : the most fearful, often mortal, wounds being made by the clashing, knife-like teeth. A sow with young is equally courageous. The sows construct nests of grass in dense covert or bushy hillsides, in much the same manner as described under Giant Forest Hog. Their most deadly natural enemy is the leopard, and where leopards have been exterminated Bush Pig always become a serious menace to all cultivation. Their habits and the nature of their habitat, render them most difficult to control.

In nature, they perform a valuable role by constantly furrowing and turning over the soil, destroying numerous insect larvae and grubs, and by aiding seed dispersal.

Their heavier, more typically pig-like form, thickly bristled coats, and the fact that they run with the tail down, should distinguish them in the field from Warthog. The Bush Pigs differ from true pigs by only having 42, instead of 44, teeth. They are wide spread throughout Africa.

3. WARTHOG

Phacochoerus aethiopicus aeliani   (Cretzcshmar)

(Kiswahili : *Ngiri*)

Field Impression.—A naked-skinned wild pig with merely bristly hairs down back of neck and shoulders. Conspicuous warts protrude on either side of the face below the eyes, and the upper tusks are large and widely upward-curved. Moves about by day in fairly open country, in pairs or family parties, and when trotting raises the tail stiffly upwards over the rump, the extreme tip wobbling about loosely.

Descriptive Notes.—The warthog is the commonest wild pig of the African plains and savannas. The males are larger and heavier than the sows, and grow far bigger and more widespread upper tusks. The young are plain-coloured at birth. Generally of a dull grey colour (varied with the colour of the local soil—as they are great wallowers), the Warthog usually has a few stiff whitish bristles sprouting backwards from the cheeks (longer and more conspicuous in the young), otherwise, save for the coppery-black bristles sprouting from neck and shoulders in the form of an erectile mane, and the long double tuft at the end of the slender tail, its hide is naked, except for a few short, sparse bristles. Enormous wart-like protuberances project from the face, more grotesquely than in either Bush Pig or Forest Hog. Body length about 3 feet. Tail about 12 inches. Shoulder height about 30 inches. Weight 210 lbs, generally about 180-200 lbs. The ears are without tufts at their tips.

WART HOG

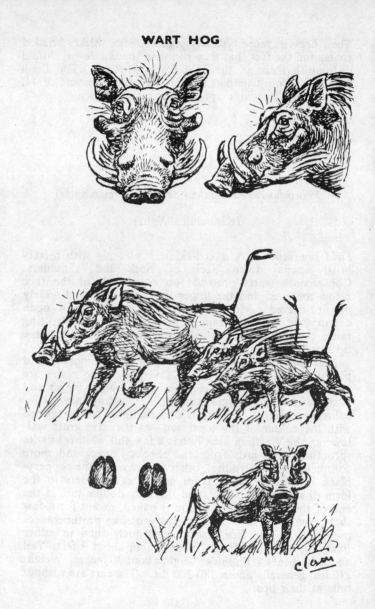

Tusks.—The upper tusks are extremely massive and long, widely curved upwards at tips, and are used mainly for digging. Up to 25 inches in length in East Africa. The lower tusks, which are sharp and used for fighting, self-defence, etc., are rarely more than 6 inches in length.

Distribution.—Common, and easily seen in Nairobi National Park, Amboseli National Reserve, Tsavo N.P. (East and West), Mara N.R., and Marsabit N.R.; occurs in the Mountain National Parks.

Habits.—The Warthog is the most readily observed of all the wild pigs, and in most general game areas it is common. Being a diurnal feeder, it can be seen moving about at all hours of the day, and usually drinks towards mid-day. Warthog are not so gregarious as bush pig, and are seldom seen other than in family parties (a boar and sow and three or four or more youngsters as a rule); in pairs or singly, though several parties may associate at a drinking place or mud-wallow. They are always most entertaining to watch, especially when boar, sow and several youngsters are running along fast, all their long thin tails stiffly erect with only the tufted tips wobbling about. They feed on grass and roots of all kinds, wild fruits, etc., and are not as a rule destructive to cultivated crops. The large upper tusks are used mainly for digging out bulbous roots. When doing this, a warthog kneels on his front legs, and adopts the same attitude when drinking. On the whole they are silent creatures, only uttering soft grunts occasionally as they feed, and a long-drawn grunt of alarm before running away. Bush pigs, on the other hand, constantly utter a deep long-drawn grunting as they feed or move about. Although courageous when wounded or attacked, warthog are peaceably disposed creatures, not half as aggressive or pugnacious as bush pig.

Warthogs usually lie up in old antbear or other burrows, and take refuge in these when chased by dogs or cheetah. They usually swing round and back into such refuges tail-first, and have been known to come out in double-quick time when a porcupine happened to be in residence! The principal enemies of the Warthog are lion, leopard, cheetah and wild dog.

THE CARNIVORA (LARGE)

LION

Panthera leo massaica (Neumann)

(Kiswahili : *Simba*)

Descriptive Notes.—General appearance well-known, but in the East African Lion the darker spots present on the flanks and limbs of cubs remain more frequently (to a certain extent) in adults—particularly lionesses—than in South Africa. The body colour varies from a silvery-grey above to dark ochre-brown, the underparts always being paler—almost white in lionesses, and buffy-ochre in adult males. Black marks form a band across the back of the ear, and the tail tuft (which is peculiar to the lion among all the Cats) is also black. The size and colour of the mane in the male vary greatly. Some male lions grow very large, handsome manes which completely cover the shoulders, and extend backwards in the form of an impressive ridge between the shoulder blades; others grow merely a longer or shorter "ruff" round the neck; while yet others may be practically maneless—but all males have a well-defined, usually yellowish ruff of long hair round the cheeks, and this begins to grow early in life, and should always enable a young, or practically maneless, male lion to be distinguished easily from a lioness who never grows any such ruff or side-whiskers. The forepaws of a lion are much larger and broader than his hind ones, whereas in the lioness the difference is not so prcnounced—hence the spoor of a male is always much larger than that of a female. The male stands higher at the shoulder, and is larger and heavier generally, than the female. The cubs are covered with dark brindlings (vertical) on body, and large, dark "rosette"-like spots on the flanks and limbs, and dusky bands on the tail (which at first has no pro-

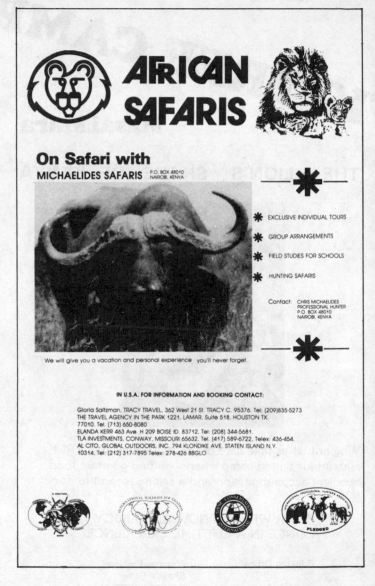

(LARGE CARNIVORA) **LION**

♂

♀

YOUNG
MALE

HEAVY
MANED
MALE

nounced tuft), but these markings tend to disappear, more or less, as maturity approaches.

Length of an average adult male, a little under 9 feet from tip of nose to tip of tail (including the curious horny appendage concealed in the tuft). A really fine one about 9 feet 4 inches, and an exceptionally large one 9 feet 6 inches.

Colonel Stevenson-Hamilton, whose measurements I quote, states that among 150 lions he has measured carefully in the course of his experience he has only once taped a lion "which even approached 10 feet in length." Females average about a foot less than males. *Weight* of a big male with full stomach up to 500 lbs; without stomach-contents, probably under 400 lbs. A big lioness weighs about one hundred pounds less than a male.

Shoulder height, males, between 3 feet 4 inches and 3 feet 9 inches. Lionesses average about 2 feet 10 inches.

Distribution.—There are usually up to 40 lions in Nairobi National Park, where they are easily seen. They occur fairly plentifully in Tsavo N.P. (East and West), Amboseli and Mara National Reserves, and Marsabit N.R. Lions seldom occur in the Mountain Forest National Parks.

Habits.—The lion, as befits the "King of Beasts," is always the greatest attraction to those who wish to see the wonderful fauna of Africa; and fortunately, of the larger cats, he is the most easily seen in the Parks and Reserves. Although decidedly nocturnal in areas where they are constantly hunted or disturbed, lions frequently move abroad, and even hunt, by day in national parks, and probably more has been learnt of their natural habits since the institution of these parks than at any previous period. During the heat of the day (from about 10 a.m. till about 4 p.m.) lions usually lie down and sleep in some shady nook, or under bush, unless it is a cool, wet, or cloudy day, when they are not at all easily located unless a very sharp look out is maintained for a glimpse of extended tawny forms half-concealed in the grass.

In the very early mornings, or in the cool of the afternoon, they wander about more freely, and of course they hunt all night (when hungry). They are indolent, lazy creatures, and prefer as little exertion as possible : so that if they can find suitable carrion they will not bother to hunt, and they will return again and again to a kill, as long

The practical way to get your message across.

MORE SPACE
PRIVACY
CHEAPER TO SEND
PERFORATION LINE for
EASY OPENING
2 FULL COLOUR PICTURES
APPROVED BY THE KENYA POST OFFICE

BY AIRMAIL
PAR AVION

2/:
POSTAGE
WORLDWIDE

now on sale everywhere!

AEROGRAMME by *FOTOFORM*

the aerogramme postcards

as anything eatable remains—no matter how "high" or maggot-infested! When really hungry, lions become extremely bold and determined, and will stop at nothing to obtain their prey, and are then the reverse of the lazy, good-natured looking creatures which they appear to be when content. Normally they prey mainly upon the larger antelopes and zebra, ostriches, and buffalo, and occasionally giraffe, but when really hungry nothing is too small or insignificant for them to catch and devour, and even man himself may fall a victim under such circumstances if opportunity is available. "Man-eating" is fortunately rare among lions generally; not, I think, because they do not like the taste of human flesh, but rather because throughout the centuries they have learnt to fear and avoid the human scent. Even when a wounded lion mauls his human opponent to death, he usually leaves the carcass untouched. On the other hand, once a lion has tasted human flesh, and found how easily man can be stalked and killed, he very quickly becomes a confirmed man-eater unless he is destroyed : and, in the case of a lioness, if her cubs are raised on such fare, they will take to man-eating as naturally as any other form of prey. However, the vast majority of lions are purely game killers, or cattle killers, and invariably leave man alone, and avoid him as far as possible. If encountered in the bush, when one is on foot, Lions nearly always bolt, or at least walk away, and if not molested they are seldom dangerous—particularly by day.

However, like all highly intelligent animals, they are very subject to individual temperament and character and one cannot generalise. Although seemingly phlegmatic, Lions are very nervous and highly-strung, and their mood can change with astonishing rapidity. The slightest unusual happening—such as a person foolishly getting out of a car, at close quarters with a lazily dozing pride, to get a better photograph, will at once transform the latter into defensively-growling "yellow" perils who, though they will most likely bolt, may also rush at object of alarm in self-defence. It cannot be sufficiently emphasised that though lions in National Parks can be quite safely approached as closely as one likes in a motor car (even lionesses with small cubs), and appear to betray no emotion other than mild, tolerant curiosity (cars are not dangerous, in their experience, and they obviously don't look—still less smell—good to eat), they are in reality potentially highly dangerous and very powerful beasts; and one should keep reasonably quiet and avoid sudden jerky movements (and certainly on no account attempt to get out) in their close presence. Whether they simply do not recognise the rightful identity of human beings in cars (they appear to look straight at you, and obviously follow movements) or have come to learn that human beings in cars are harmless, is still not understood. Under any other circumstances, a lioness with small cubs is proverbially dangerous, and liable to attack anything or anybody in their supposed defence. She will permit her offspring to gnaw at and sniff at the wheels of a motionless car, meanwhile serenely dozing near-by—but with ever watchful yellow eyes.

Lions are more gregarious than most cats, and associate in prides, sometimes up to thirty or more, though usually from about four to five or fifteen. Old males frequently hunt in pairs, and are sometimes found singly. The Lionesses usually do the actual killing (except in case of heavier beasts like buffalo), the males usually driving the game, by scent or by roaring, towards the former who are lying in concealment. They are most intelligently co-operative. The prey is killed as a rule either by a bite in the throat from the front (strangulation), or by jumping on to the back of a fleeing antelope, when the front paw seizes and pulls in the muzzle, causing the animal to fall forward on to its neck which is usually automatically broken. I have seen a Lion jump on to a galloping zebra from the flank, knock it over, and as it fell seize its throat in a stranglehold. Young Lions are assisted and taught by the Lioness : to begin with on half-killed small animals, such as warthog, which she holds down while the cubs "kill" it! Gruesome, and painful to watch, but necessary training! Later on, when about eighteen months old, they are allowed to do the killing, and frequently not only make a bungling job of it but get roughly handled—even seriously injured, by the victim itself who may escape and even charge its assailant! A Lion's training is a hard one, and it has to amass considerable knowledge of the habits and movements of the game on which it must live, if it is to survive.

Lions are polygamous, and several Lionesses may associate with one big male and bear his cubs, while not uncommonly two big males may mate with the same lioness without friction—though as a rule the most powerful male drives away his rivals, and sometimes mortal fights ensue. Usually, a mating pair spends a regular "Honeymoon" : remaining together in one small area for several days, during which they will not hunt, being completely absorbed in each other. At such times a male Lion may be irritable and inclined to "show off"; and he may growl threateningly at a halted car, lash his tail, and perhaps even make a rush or two in the car's direction. The tail, and the ears, are most expressive. When really angry, a Lion (either sex) will flatten its ears, growling and grunting hoarsely, at the same time twitching its tail-tip from side to side, ever more rapidly in proportion to its mounting rage. At the point of charging, the tail is jerked and swung up and down, and finally erected rigidly above the back, when the Lion usually comes at a fast gallop. If the tail is twitching or jerking, but the ears are still cocked, the animal is merely nervous or excited, and not angry. The full-throated roaring, which is lovely to hear, is usually uttered after killing—to summon others of the pride : on the way to or from drinking (after feeding) and for sheer joy of life, or when driving game. Short coughing grunts may be used during the drive, and take the place of roaring in disturbed country. When calling to each other, Lions use soft, barely audible, throaty sounds : and small cubs "hiccough" and make harsh "miauuing" sounds. The cubs, from 2 to 4 as a rule, are born in thickets or patches of reeds or dwarf palms, etc. A Lioness usually breeds every two years, as the cubs are still unable to fend for themselves until about eighteen months old. Lionesses will take it in turns to act as nurse-guards to each others' cubs.

The mane of the male becomes evident in about his third year : previous to that it is indicated by the shaggier hair on cheeks and throat, and usually a budding tuft on the forehead. Manes vary from black and brown, to fair, and are most commonly a mixture, darker at top and sides.

LEOPARD

Panthera pardus pardus (Linnaeus)

(Kiswahili : *Chui*)

Field Impression.—Differs from the more commonly seen Cheetah by being lower on the leg and more powerfully built. Its finer-set coat is closely marked with irregularly-shaped *groups* of spots—forming "rosettes" on body and broken "bars" across the chest. Tail very long, and often upcurled at tip.

Descriptive Notes.—Unlike the cheetah, which has blunt, only semi-retractile claws, the Leopard is a true cat which can sheathe its powerful, curved claws except when they are actually in use. The spots on the head are small and solid and very closely set, but on the shoulders and body they are set more widely apart and combined in rosette-like clusters or circles, become solid again, though large on hindquarters and abdomen. The tail is spotted and the tip is usually black. Whiskers very long and bristly. Ears black above with white tips. The eyes, which are fierce and baleful looking, are greenish yellow : and the colour of the upper portion of the body generally is rich golden-yellow with white on throat, chest, and underparts. The centres of the rosettes are usually darker in ground colour than the surrounding area. Teeth and jaw, more powerful than those of cheetah. The male is larger than the female, and a large male may measure as much as 7 feet 6 inches from tip of nose to end of tail, while several have been recorded of 8 feet and over. Mostly they are 7 feet, or slightly under. The heaviest recorded East African Leopard (Roosevelt) weighed 130 lbs., but the average weight is probably between 100 and 120 lbs.— females average from 20—30 lbs. less. Average shoulder height about 28 inches. The cubs are born with rather dark, woolly fur, the spots at first being indistinct.

Black Leopards are rarer in Africa than in Malaya (where they are most common) but several have been obtained in Kenya—mostly in the Aberdare and Mount Kenya forests. In this melanistic form, the coat is very dark glossy brown—

LEOPARD AND CHEETAH

LEOPARD

CHEETAH

Clau
'58.

141

practically black—but the normal markings are more or less evident in the pelage.

Distribution.—Leopards occur in all the National Parks and National Reserves of Kenya, but owing to their secretive, nocturnal habits, they are rarely seen.

Habits.—Unlike the cheetah, which is more or less diurnal, and favours open, or semi-open, country, the leopard is a nocturnal hunter. He favours dense bush or thickets or true forest, and in the more low-lying or bush country is most plentiful along wooded margins of streams, etc. The Leopards inhabiting the high mountain forests are usually larger, with more handsomely marked coats, than those of the scrub or plains' areas. He obtains his prey by stealth, ambush, or dropping on to it from a tree (he is an excellent climber), whereas the cheetah chases his prey like a greyhound.

Leopards are solitary animals, never more than a pair inhabiting a specific range—though temporarily they may be accompanied by the contemporary young. Males frequently lead a solitary life except when they associate with a female for breeding purposes. They hunt over a wide area of their chosen range; seldom remaining in one portion of it for more than a few days, say a week, at a time, before moving on, and so, in the course of a month or so, patrolling the whole beat. This is no doubt in order to relax the vigilance of the local prey. As long as they are not disturbed, and the beat harbours plenty of prey, leopards will remain there for years. They prey on medium-sized and small antelopes, and the young of larger buck; together with monkeys, baboons, game birds and others, cane rats, hyrax, and smaller animals of all types, and, in fact, will tackle anything they can overpower when hungry. They are probably the principal natural enemies of bush pigs, baboons, and monkeys, and should rightly receive a measure of protection in areas where the latter are too numerous. Conversely, where the leopard has been exterminated these agricultural pests often prove a grave problem. Monkeys and baboons will often betray the movements of a Leopard, by coughing or barking clamourously whenever they catch sight of him, and they will follow him along in the branches overhead.

The Leopard is, on the whole, a silent animal—particularly in settled areas where he is frequently hunted. In undisturbed areas, however, he quite frequently gives utterance to an extremely harshly grating, grunting cough, uttered several times in rapid succession. After each grunt, the breath is drawn in huskily : the whole producing a double effect, aptly likened to the sound of coarse wood being sawn : something like, *Grunt-ha! Grunt-ha! Grunt-ha! Grunt-ha!*—usually ending in a harsh sighing note. At times I have heard them utter a short roar—apparently as a greeting between two individuals. An angry Leopard growls and coughs like a similarly disposed lion.

For his size and weight, a Leopard is probaby one of the most dangerous of animals. Normally shy and retiring, and always seeking safety by stealth and rarely attacking (except at very close quarters) when unmolested; a wounded leopard will charge almost for certain as soon as his place of concealment is approached, and so determined and courageous is he that it is rarely that he can be stopped except by death. He moves very fast, is low on the ground, and his attack in such circumstances is usually to "scalp" his aggressor with the fearful claws. As in Asia, the African Leopard has a curious liking for dog flesh, and many a dog, even to the size of a Great Dane, has been snatched and devoured by a Leopard. In spite of this, during the day a Leopard is easily "treed" by dogs. In the early mornings Leopards like to sun themselves on antheaps, or slabs of rock, or open places, before retiring into covert for the day, and these are the times when one has the best chances of seeing them. They often haunt rocky, boulder-clad hillocks, where the numerous hyrax form an easy prey.

Sometimes you may notice a portion of the carcase of a buck hanging high up, wedged in the branches of a tree. This is a sign of a Leopard's presence, as they will so larder their prey to preserve it from the attention of hyenas, jackals, or lions. The cubs are born in caves or rock crevices, or in dense thickets, and are usually two or three in number. The gestation period is three months. The spoor is much like that of a lion in shape, but narrower, and very much smaller.

CHEETAH

Acinonyx jubatus raineyi (Heller)

(Kiswahili : *Duma*)

Field Impression.—About as long as a leopard, but higher on the leg, with a wirier coat and incipient, short mane on back of shoulders. Lanky and rather hollow-backed, carries its short head low as it walks and has pronounced long black "tear" lines from front of eyes to muzzle. Body spots small, round, and solid—dotted regularly all over body and flanks but more sparsely on head. Tail ringed at end with a white tip.

Descriptive Notes.—The Cheetah, or Hunting Leopard, is not a true cat (which has sheathable, curved claws). Its claws are blunt like those of a dog, and can only be partially withdrawn, so that Cheetah spoor, in size much like that of leopard, can be distinguished by the indication of the claw tips. The head is smaller and rounder than that of a leopard, with shorter ears. The eyes are yellowish brown, large, and mild in expression, and the teeth are weaker. The coat is more wiry, and the spots dotted about singly, not in clusters. The tail is spotted for the greater part of its length, then becomes decidedly banded or ringed with black near the end, while the tip is fairly bushy and white. The long dark lines extending from front corners of eyes to sides of upper lip are very conspicuous and entirely characteristic. The sexes are alike, though males are larger than females and grow a more extensive "ruff" on top of shoulders. The small cubs are at first smoky-grey, with hardly any markings, and very rough coats. Later they become yellowish on flanks and limbs, and the spots gradually become more distinct. Adults are tawny-yellow, or sandy-rufous in ground colour—much paler than leopards—becoming white on underparts and round mouth, throat and chest, and inside the legs. *Shoulder height*, 2 feet 6 inches to 3 feet. Average length of a male about 7 feet (a Kenya record is 7 feet 9 inches), of which the tail is about 2 feet 7 inches. *Weight*, from 90 lbs. to 136½ lbs.

Distribution.—It occurs in Nairobi National Park, where it is often seen singly or in pairs. It is reasonably common in Tsavo National Park (both sections), Amboseli N.R., Mara N.R., and Marsabit N.R. It does not occur in the Mountain Forest National Parks. Cheetah are nowhere very numerous, but well distributed over most game areas.

Habits.—although it is not nearly so commonly distributed as the leopard, the Cheetah, being diurnal in habit, is far more frequently *seen*. In fact, after the lion, it is the most often observed of the larger cats, and it is very frequently mistaken for leopard. As described above, such mistakes can be avoided by noticing the different type of spots, build, coat, and so on. Its method of hunting is entirely peculiar to its species, and unique among the cat-like creatures. It is built for speed, and, after stalking as close as possible to its chosen prey, it races after the latter, finally seizing it by the throat and causing death by strangulation. It is a "sprinter," however, and cannot maintain this great speed for more than 100 yards or so, and if the victim has successfully eluded it by that time, it usually gives up the chase. For such a limited distance, the Cheetah is considered to be the fastest mammal, and its all-out speed has been recorded at from 60-70 miles per hour. A pair of Cheetahs will combine in chase to outwit the nimble little steenbok, or dik-dik, as they twist and turn and "jink" distractingly in flight.

Cheetah usually prey on the medium and smaller antelopes, and females and young of larger antelopes. They also hunt warthog and game birds and smaller things.

Contrary to the naturally savage leopard, the Cheetah is a mild-natured animal, rarely attacking its aggressor even when wounded—in any case it has no vicious hooked claws, and can only bite. It is easily tamed, and makes a fascinating and fairly reliable pet, and is naturally affectionate. When angered, or cornered, or wounded, it will growl deeply, but otherwise utters a curious, bird-like chirruping note, and purrs deeply when pleased. Owing to its hunting method, the Cheetah avoids dense bush or forest, and is only found in comparatively open country or on grassy plains.

Two to four cubs are born, and these are at first marked only on the limbs and lower portions of the otherwise greyish bodies, and the infantile fur is long and woolly. Cheetahs are usually seen singly, or in pairs, but as many as five or six are sometimes seen together and these are probably family parties, which break up later.

SPOTTED HYENA

Crocuta crocuta germinans (Matschie)

(Kiswahili : *Fisi*)

Field Impression.—About as big as a large, powerful dog, but with very sloping back : large rounded ears, and rather short bushy tail. Reddish to drab grey : the body covered with large more or less oval dark spots. Front of face black. A slight, forward-directed mane along back of neck from shoulders. Jaws very massive.

Descriptive Notes.—The hyenas apparently form a link between the "cats" and the "dogs", although pertaining more to the latter in general characters. They have the most powerful jaws of all living mammals, with enormously powerful carnassial teeth which enable them to crack the toughest bones. They are mainly nocturnal, feeding very largely on carrion, and the abandoned kills of lions and other carnivora, but also kill sickly or badly wounded animals and newly-born young of all kinds. The Spotted Hyena of Africa is the largest and most powerful of the hyenas, and can easily be recognised by its wiry but short coat, spotted colouration, and large, upstanding, but very rounded ears—shaped not unlike those of a lion. The body colour varies a good deal, from a pale grey through drab to rufous-ochre : but in all cases the body is marked with large solid round or oval black or brown spots. The large, rather wistful eyes are dark brown, and the nostrils are very broad. Young animals are at first dark, the spots appearing as the coat lightens and the coat much longer than in an adult. Shoulder height 2 feet 3 inches—3 feet. Total length over 5 feet. Weight up to 170 lb.

Distribution.—Common in Nairobi and Tsavo National Parks, and in Amboseli, Mara, and Marsabit National Reserves. Not found much in forest country.

Habits.—The Spotted Hyena is one of the most "typical" dwellers in the African Wilds. His eerie, rather hideous wailing-howl begins in a low, often hoarse note which, rising gradually ends in an abrupt high-pitched one ("*Auweeoo! Ooo-we! Ooo-we!*"). It is the commonest of nocturnal sounds around any Safari camp and used, not so long ago, to be frequently heard in Nairobi itself at night.

In addition to this ordinary call, which is used as a means of communication, the Spotted Hyena gives utterance to

SPOTTED HYENA

an astonishing variety of grunts, growls, and chuckles at various times which often mystify the human listener: and when excited, as at mating time, or when being chased about by lions at a kill, it utters a rising and falling series of chattering howls which resemble peals of maniacal laughter —certainly the most eerie of all its cries, and which has earned for it the name of Laughing Hyena. As it utters this laughing cry, a Spotted Hyena usually raises and spreads its short bushy tail.

Hyenas are mainly nocturnal, hiding away during the day in clumps of bush, underground hollows, etc., but start to prowl during the late afternoon, and may often be seen then and during the early morning hours : while they will gather at a lion's kill, and may wait about there throughout the day. Normally they are solitary, or seen in pairs or family parties, but they gather at a carcass, and when really hungry sometimes combine in packs, at which times they may attack and pull down quite large antelopes if such can be cornered. Spotted Hyenas are big, powerful brutes, and through normally cowardly can, on occasions, become exceedingly bold and aggressive at night. I have had one almost snatch a pan of eggs and bacon out of my hand in the darkness, and natives sleeping unprotected in the bush at night have often had part of the face, or a limb, bitten off by a Spotted Hyena. They can crack the heaviest bones, and so get at the marrow, swallowing bits of bone in the process, and this bony diet results in their droppings drying pure white and so being easily distinguishable in the veld.

There is a prevalent belief that the Hyena is hermaphrodite, and that the sexes are indistinguishable. This is not so, and the cause of this misapprehension lies in the fact that the external labial swellings in the female are unusually developed, and at a glance may easily be mistaken for the scrotum of the male.

As you see the Spotted Hyena slouching along at his clumsy, ungainly gait through the veld, with his massive head and long neck held low, his back sloping sharply to the hindquarters, and his whole attitude conveying a suggestion of shame-faced, "hang-dog", cowardice which seems grotesque in so powerful an animal, you would hardly realise that many a fine lion or lioness, when crippled with age or wounds, is gradually followed and watched and finally pulled down and torn to pieces by this scavenger. During its youth and prime, the lion hates and despises the Spotted Hyena more than any of the other scavengers (jackal, vulture and marabou) which assemble at its kill to wait the opportunity to feed on what remains. He is reasonably tolerant of the active little jackals, but the Hyena he seems really to loathe, and this I think may be due to an instinctive fear of what, sooner or later, may prove to be his fate. Many an unguarded lion cub has been devoured by Hyenas.

Hyenas have also been noticed scooping fish out of shallow pools. There is no doubt that they intelligently observe the movements of vultures, gazing skywards to note in which direction they are converging, in order to ascertain the position of a distant carcass. Their scenting powers are remarkably efficient.

In spite of their rather objectionable role, the scavengers of the veld perform a very useful function in disposing rapidly of festering carcasses in the tropical sun, and the Hyena may truly be regarded as nature's dustbin! Their gruesome habits, and unearthly cries, have caused Hyenas to be associated by primitive Africans with witches who are believed to ride about at night on Hyenas, and frequently to turn temporarily into these creatures while performing their nefarious activities!

The young, usually two, are born in old antbear holes, or other such places.

STRIPED HYENA

Hyaena hyaena dubbah (Meyer)

(The Kiswahili *Fisi* seems to apply to both species of Hyena)

Field Impression.—Rather smaller and slighter in build than the Spotted Hyena, the Striped Hyena can be recognised by its very pointed, upright ears, shaggy erectile mane along back, more bushy tail, and vertical black stripes on a greyish ground. Front of face, black.

Descriptive Notes.—The Striped Hyena has a longer coat than the Spotted species : particularly long on shoulders and back, and the long narrow pointed ears are quite different. The bushy tail is slightly longer, but blunt-tipped. Grey in ground colour, it is marked with black vertical stripes on shoulders and hindquarters while the upper parts of the limbs and chest have horizontal black bars. Front of face and throat black. Total length about 54 inches. Height about 30 inches at shoulder.

Distribution.—A much rarer animal than the Spotted Hyena, this species, being very nocturnal, is less easily seen. It is rare in Nairobi National Park, and occurs in

in Tsavo National Park (East and West—"Reported but not seen" in the West), Amboseli National Reserve and Marsabit National Reserve. Not recorded yet from Mara N.R. I was fortunate in seeing a very fine specimen at Amboseli.

Habits.—The Striped Hyena—like the leopard—is common to both Asia and Africa, with slight local differences. In Africa it is not found south of the Kilimanjaro area, its place south of that being taken by the closely related Brown Hyena (*H. Brunnea*). Everywhere in its range it appears to be a rarer animal than the Spotted Hyena, and it is very much more strictly nocturnal and solitary, so that records of its habits and distribution are less easy to obtain. It is rather higher on the leg than the Spotted Hyena, but has the same steep slope from shoulder to rump and a similar walking action. The pointed ears and shoulder crest are very noticeable.

On the whole, little seems to have been recorded about the habits of the Striped Hyena in Africa. It is stated to be more of a decided carrion eater, and far less audacious or aggressive than the more powerful Spotted Hyena, and to be rather timid in disposition generally. The first specimen of a Striped Hyena from East Africa which reached Europe was apparently trapped by the German naturalist C. G. Schillings on the banks of Lake Natron, between Kilimanjaro and Victoria Nyanza in 1896. Schillings also records the native name for this hyena as "Kingugua". Certain odd specimens are said to attack sheep or goats occasionally. I have never heard the call of the Striped Hyena, but it has been described as an unearthly moan or shriek. It is probably more plentiful than suspected in suitable areas as is the case with many strictly nocturnal, retiring types of animals.

AFRICAN HUNTING DOG ("WILD DOG")

Lycaon pictus lupinus (Thomas.)

(Kiswahili : *Mbwa mwitu.*)

Field Impression.—About as large as an Alsatian, but more slenderly and wirily built with more massive jaws and shorter muzzle. Ears very large and upstanding, oval or rounded. Tail bushy, with usually a pronounced white terminal half. Body colouration mostly black, with patches of sandy-rufous and white markings—a curious blotchy colouration. Associates in packs of various sizes, but sometimes noted singly or in fours or fives, etc.

Descriptive Notes.—Most characteristic are the very large upstanding ears with decidedly rounded tips, and the

INNER
RIGHT
FORE

ABSENCE
OF
5th TOE
IN LYCAON

white tip to the fairly long bushy tail (though it is usually white, occasionally the tip is darker coloured, but there is always some white in the tail). In East Africa the Hunting Dog seems to be much darker as a whole than the South African races : the black and white portions predominating, most commonly, with sandy-rufous mainly round the upper part of head, back of neck, and an odd fleck here and there : whereas in the South African races the colouration is more evenly distributed, and the sandy-rufous patches more extensive. However, the species is notable for its individual variation, and no two dogs in any one pack are marked exactly alike. The puppies and younger animals are usually blacker, on the whole, than older specimens. Front of face and muzzle (below the eyes) backs of ears, and throat ruff usually black—also a central line down the forehead from between the ears. The limbs, which are thin and very muscular, are mostly white, with black markings. The African Hunting Dog differs from the true dogs by having only four toes to each foot (it lacks the "Dewclaw"). It is a unique species. There is a prominent ruff of longer hair on the throat. Shoulder height 2—2 feet 6 inches. Overall length up to 4 feet 10 inches. Tail about 1 foot 2 inches. Weight 60—80 lb.

Distribution.—Wild Dogs occur in all the principal game areas, but not in forest country, and may be seen if one is fortunate. They range over large tracts of country, and constantly move from one area of their range to another as game soon becomes very wild when they are about, thus to encounter them is always very much a matter of chance.

Habits.—These are the most ruthless and interesting animal hunters in Africa. The packs vary from a few individuals to as many as 40, and they hunt their quarry with most intelligent co-operation. They decide on what animal they wish to pursue out of a herd, and then stick to it remorselessly : one or two dogs chasing it hard, and the remainder jogging along comfortably in the rear, or spread out on either flank. As the first two tire, others take their place, and so on; until, hopelessly wearied, the selected victim begins to lose pace, when the pack closes in, biting chunks out of it until it finally falls from weakness and loss of blood when it is usually disposed of in a few minutes, and very little, save bones, left. The usual prey consists of medium and small antelopes, such as impala, reedbuck, gazelles, steenbok, etc., and the females and young of waterbuck, kudu, kongoni, and so on : but occasionally larger male antelopes are also pursued and pulled down, while they have been known to chase lions off their kill. On the other hand, spotted hyena have been seen to chase Wild Dogs away from their own kill! (Kruger National Park).

In spite of their liking for dog flesh, leopards will at once give way to Wild Dogs, and seek refuge in a tree! Wild Dogs seldom eat carrion and invariably kill their own prey, and as nothing is ever left of it (unless they are disturbed) they never return to a kill. They have rarely been known to attack man, though they are very inquisitive, and will run in circles round a human wayfarer, barking in deep, hoarse tones, and jumping up and down to peer at him through the grass, before galloping on ahead to repeat the performance.

The hunt is usually conducted in silence, though the actual kill is accompanied by curious chattering sounds and whimpers of excitement. A short howl, bell-like in tone and rapidly repeated—a sort of *hoo-hoo-hoo*—is uttered usually at night or in the early mornings or evenings as members of a pack call to one another if separated. The bark of alarm or surprise is deeper and hoarser in tone than that of an ordinary dog, and is frequently accompanied by short growls. The rather hyena-like appearance of these animals—although there is no pronounced slope to the back and they are far more active and speedy than hyenas— was responsible for the old name of "Hyena Dog".

The bitches leave the main pack at breeding time, and several of them give birth to their pups in one breeding earth with several entrances. After weaning, they feed the pups by regurgitating semi-digested food for them, and when the pups are old enough the mothers with their young rejoin the pack. As many as 8—10 pups have been found in one breeding earth, but these are probably the progeny of two or three bitches. In the western Tsavo Park about six Wild Dogs were encountered chasing a warthog in the late afternoon, but the arrival of our car distracted the pursuers, and the wild pig made good his escape!

Hunting Dogs have a most unpleasant natural odour, something like that of old, rotten uncured animal hides.

Game are not always so wildly terrified of them as popular accounts suggest and (as they do with lions) seem to know whether the dogs are out to hunt or not. I once watched a pack of about a dozen which had just pulled down and eaten an impala. Thereafter they played and gambolled about together in the road before setting off, in carefree manner towards a small herd of waterbuck cows and calves. The latter merely watched them, and, as they came nearer, quietly trotted in single file to one side where they watched the dogs move past.

CARACAL

THE CARNIVORA (SMALL)

CARACAL, OR AFRICAN LYNX

Caracal caracal nubicus (Fischer)

(Kiswahili : *Simba mangu*)

Field Impression.—A large, rufous-coloured wild cat, with long tufts of hair projecting from the tips of its rather pointed, black-backed ears, and comparatively short tail. Its bright reddish colour (without markings) and size render it peculiarly liable to be mistaken for a steenbok when seen indistinctly in longish grass.

Descriptive Notes.—Like all the smaller wild cats, the Caracal is nocturnal, and not often seen by day. Its short fur is a rather grizzled rufous, sometimes with a greyish tinge but quite often a beautiful bay colour above, and quite unmarked. The chin and throat and upper lip (latter bordered with black) are white, and the white of the abdomen is usually stippled with small indistinct rufous spots. There is a dark spot above each eye, and the large but narrow and pointed ears are black behind and fringed with white in front—their extreme tips ornamented with long, narrow tufts of hair which frequently droop downwards. Tail short and slender, only about nine inches in length. Eyes very brilliant, rich amber-yellow, sometimes with a greenish tint. *Shoulder height* 16—18 inches. *Length* about 26—30 inches. *Weight* about 40 lb.

Distribution.—The Caracal occurs in Nairobi National Park, but is not common, and rarely seen. It is sparsely distributed in Mara and Amboseli and Marsabit National Reserves, and reported as fairly common in Tsavo National Park. Nowhere, however, is it as plentiful a species as it is in parts of South Africa.

Habits.—This is the most powerful and fierce of the smaller cats, and an exceedingly handsome beast. Its character is much like that of a leopard, and like the latter it will take refuge in a tree when pursued by dogs. Caracals are solitary as a rule, though the sexes associate during breeding periods. They prey on the smaller antelopes, hares, birds of all kinds, and have been said to attack sitting ostriches. In addition, they prey on many smaller kinds of creatures.

Stevenson-Hamilton records cases of both Tawny Eagle and Martial Eagle being killed at night, while roosting, by Caracal. Caracal certainly move about by day more often than most of the other wild cats, and at such times their rufous colouring easily causes them to be mistaken for small buck such as steenbok. In the early mornings, or late afternoons, there is always a chance of seeing one. Two or three kittens are usually born at a time, and these may be born in a disused antbear hole, or in the hollow of a tree, or a cleft between rocks.

SERVAL

Felis serval hindei (Wroughton)

(Kiswahili : *Mondo*)

Field Impression.—A large wild cat, rather tall on the leg, with large oval ears (upstanding), small face, and rather short tail. Rich tawny-yellow, marked with large rather widely separated black spots which tend to form bars along the back and round chest. Backs of ears black, with white centres. Colouration to a certain extent resembles that of a cheetah.

Descriptive Notes.—The outstanding characteristics of the Serval are its very large, upstanding ears, and comparatively small, very cat-like face. It looks a "leggy" creature; rather emphasised by its rather short, ringed tail. It is undoubtedly the most handsome of the smaller African cats, as well as one of the largest. Height about 20 inches. Length about 54 inches : Weight about 34 lb. Black specimens have been obtained in Kenya. The spots are large and oval, in normal specimens, fairly widely separated running in well-marked lines along the back and across the shoulders.

Distribution.—The Serval is recorded from all the Kenya National Parks and National Reserves, and in the Aberdares*, particularly around the Tree tops salient. Nocturnal

SERVAL CAT

in habit, however, it is most likely to be seen only very early in the morning or late in the afternoon.

Habits.—A dweller in thick covert, the Serval is usually a haunter of lush margins of streams or rivers, and is most often found in such localities. At night, in such areas, its weird call may occasionally be heard—a rapidly repeated :

* Sheldrick noted a Black specimen on the moorlands at about 10,000 feet.

"*How! How! How! How!*" It preys upon guinea-fowl and other birds, hares, cane rats, the young of small antelopes, and so on. In spite of its size, it is less powerful than, and not so savage in disposition as, the Caracal. About three kittens are born at a time, often in an old antbear or porcupine hole.

GOLDEN CAT

Profelis aurata cottoni (Lydekker)

Field Impression.—A large wild cat, almost leopard-like in build, about twice the size of a domestic cat, with a moderately long tail. In colour it ranges from golden-brown to grey, with or without darker spots on flanks and underparts, and it is said sometimes to pass through several colour phases. Ears rounded with dark tips. Strictly a dweller in dense forest, and very rare in Kenya.

General Notes.—Little is recorded about this rare and beautiful cat, though it exists in the Mau and Aberdare Forests, and is likely to be seen elsewhere in Kenya. Lydekker gives its general distribution as "ranging from the Cameroons and French Congoland eastwards to the Ituri, but has been reported from Sierra Leone and perhaps Liberia." It is reported to exist on the Uganda side of the Birunga Volcanoes in the Mountain Gorilla habitat (Kigezi District.)

I can give no details of its habits, calls, etc.

TAITA GREY WILD CAT

Felis lybica taitae (Heller)

(Kiswahili : *Paka pori*)

Field Impression.—Very like an ordinary "Tabby" cat, but slightly larger and heavier and with less distinct markings on the body. Tail slightly shorter in proportion. Backs of

TAITA WILD CAT

ears rufous. Greyish above, becoming pale ochre or rufous on underparts.

Descriptive Notes.—This cat is also known as the Egyptian cat, and the "Kaffir" cat. Generally speaking, it is darker or lighter grey above, with rather indistinct wavy vertical stripes extending from the spine to the lower surface, more distinct above. The upper portions of both limbs are marked with broad dark bars, more distinct than those on the body, and there are black bars round the legs. There are tabby-like markings on the face, but the backs of the ears are rufous—and this is a useful distinguishing character. The forepart of the underparts, and chest, are spotted : but the latter or rear half of the underparts is rufous-buff and unmarked. Tail usually with black tip and two clearly defined dark rings near the tip, the remainder being marked more indistinctly. Length, 30—36 inches. Weight, 8½ lb.

Distribution.—Occurs almost everywhere, and throughout most of Africa, except in the forested areas, and occurs in all the Kenya National Parks and National Reserves except the Mountain Forest Parks.

Habits.—This is a local race of the Egyptian cat which was domesticated, deified, and often mummified, by the Ancient Egyptians; and it is considered by some authorities to be the ancestor of our domesticated cats. Being strictly nocturnal, it is not a commonly seen species—though like other night hunters it may occasionally be encountered afoot in the very early mornings or late afternoons, or in cloudy or wet weather. It looks very like a domestic tabby though somewhat larger and with more of a ruff round the cheeks.

The Wild Cat is a savage hunter, preying on birds, rodents, hares, and the young of small antelopes. It also—like its domesticated cousin—attacks and devours snakes, lizards, and other things—including insects and beetles. In settled areas it interbreeds with domestic cats : and the half-wild progeny are invariably very handsome but inclined to be untrustworthy and sometimes vicious. The call is said to be like a domestic cat's, but rather lower and harsher in tone, and rival males utter similar screeching and caterwauling serenades! About four kittens are usually born in a litter. It is fierce and untamable by nature.

CIVET

Civettictis civetta schwarzi (Cabrera)

(Kiswahili : *Fungo*)

Field Impression.—A long-bodied, rather wiry-coated animal as large as a medium-sized dog with very short, round, white-tipped ears. Black round eyes, and white round muzzle. Body covered with irregular black blotches on greyish ground, and long bushy tail rather pointed at tip which is black—sides of tail marked with black bars.

Descriptive Notes.—The African Civet stands about 15 inches at its highest point, and is about 3½ feet long—of which the tail occupies 15—18 inches. Its legs are short and slender, with non-retractible claws, but owing to the fact that its body is rather arched, and its head carried low, it appears taller on the leg than is actually the case. Its height at the back is emphasised, too, by the dorsal crest of long black hairs which can be erected at will when the animal is angered or alarmed. Its salient features are the black areas round eyes and cheeks which contrast with the white round the muzzle and upper lip, and the very short, rather rounded and white-bordered ears. The remainder of the body is clad in rather coarse, wiry hair—dark grey, sometimes with a yellowish tinge, becoming black on the abdomen and legs, and tip of long tail. Irregular, somewhat vertically directed, dark blotches mark the sides and flanks, becoming formed more like horizontal stripes on the upper parts of the limbs. The dorsal ridge of long hair is black. The long tail is bushy at its base, gradually becoming more pointed at tip. Black above, and at the tip, it is marked on the sides with black vertical stripes. There are horizontal black bars along the sides of the neck.

Distribution.—The Civet, being a most secretive, nocturnal creature, is not very often seen, though in certain localities it may be fairly common. It is recorded as rare in the Nairobi National Park; not common in either Amboseli or Mara National Reserves. In Tsavo National Park it is reported as common on Serengeti and Ziwani in the Western area, and occurs in the Eastern area : and it also occurs at Marsabit, N.R.

GENET

Habits.—This is the Civet which, housed in small cages in which it was unable to turn round, was formerly kept in large numbers in Zanzibar and the African coastal towns in order that the strong, musky contents of its scent glands could be extracted and sold commercially as "Civet"—to be used as a base for many perfumes. It is a solitary, very nocturnal creature, inhabiting bushy country at various altitudes, and lying up by day in thick grass or under thorny bushes, or in holes excavated by antbears or porcupines. Sometimes it may be noticed moving about early or late in the day, and at a distance its dark colouring makes it look black until one is near enough to see the blotchy markings. As it moves about, it carries head and tail low with the back strongly arched.

The Civet preys on small mammals and birds (up to the largest game birds) rodents, frogs and toads, and even the large terrestrial snails and millipedes which occur in such numbers during the rains. It kills hares, and no doubt the young of smaller antelope when opportunity offers. In addition to this it devours all forms of carrion, and also eats birds' eggs and wild fruits of many kinds. In fact it is omnivorous. It has the curious habit of returning regularly to the same place to deposit its droppings. It has been known to kill and devour domestic cats. Poultry left out at night (such as brooding turkeys or hens) are killed, but it is a bad climber, and cannot easily enter a strong wire-netting enclosure.

Its normal call is a series of low-pitched, throaty coughs : but when attacked or chased by dogs it growls in a deep tone. Two or three young are born at a time, usually in an old antbear hole.

NEUMANN'S GENET

Genetta genetta neumanni (Matschie)

(Kiswahili : *Kanu*)

Field Impression.—A long-bodied, lithe cat-like creature with rather narrow, pointed face and large conical ears, and very long, broadly ringed tail. The buff-grey body is marked with dark brown spots which tend to unite into longitudinal stripes along the shoulders. About as large as a cat, but lower on the legs.

Descriptive Notes.—Very catlike in form and appearance, but with noticeably longer body and shorter limbs : and with longer and narrower tail, and the face more pointed. The rather short fur of the body is drab-grey, paler below, marked with large round dark brown spots set more or less in horizontal lines or rows, becoming merged almost into disjointed stripes along the back and along the shoulders, and becoming smaller and more round along the lower portion of body and limbs. The tail is broadly ringed with dark brown, usually with a dark tip. Claws semi-retractible, curved like those of a cat. There is a white patch below each eye, and along either side of the upper lip. The body spots vary a great deal from dark brown to almost chestnut. Total length (from nose to tail tip) about 3 feet. Eyes large and amber-coloured, with vertical pupils.

Distribution.—Common in Nairobi National Park, and occurs in Tsavo National Park (east and west); Amboseli and Mara and Marsabit National reserves, and in fact almost anywhere in suitable, bushy country.

Habits.—This is another very nocturnal creature, rarely seen by day. In the dusk its attenuated, graceful form may sometimes be seen trotting across a road, or through the veld, and then the richly ringed long tail will immediately catch the eye and identify it. Genets are semi-arboreal in habit, frequently spending the day extended along a tree branch. They also lie up on anthills and among dense undergrowth, and are usually found within reasonably close proximity to water. Genets prey on anything they are capable of overpowering, and are bloodthirsty little creatures—wickedly destructive to poultry, and capable of squeezing their narrow forms through surprisingly small holes in fences or runs. They prey on hares, and smaller creatures of all sorts, birds of all kinds (attacking quite large ones at roost at night), reptiles, carrion, insects and wild fruits. They are closely related to the Civets, and differ from true cats in that their claws are only semi-retractile. 2—3 kittens are born in an underground hole or burrow, or very often in the hollow of a tree or stump. Genets can be tamed, and sometimes make delightful and affectionate pets. They are among the most beautifully marked of the smaller cat-like creatures.

Besides this, there are 2 other species of Genet in Kenya which could occur in the National Parks, but these need not be described here.

WHITE-TAILED MONGOOSE

Ichneumia albicauda ibeana (Thomas)

(Kiswahili : *Kicheche* or *nguchiro*)

Field Impression.—A large grey, rather shaggy-coated mongoose, usually with a white tail, blackish on limbs and underparts. Some specimens, however, have dark tails. Rather larger than a cat.

Descriptive Notes.—The large size (second only to the Greater Grey Mongoose, or Ichneumon) and usually white bushy tail help to identify this animal, which otherwise is grizzled-grey or brownish-grey above, blacker on limbs and underparts. The hairs of the coat are rather coarse and wiry, and the head is rather pointed and fox-like, except that, as in all mongooses, the ears are short and rounded. Length of body 22-24 inches, with about another 16 inches of tail. Weight of a large one about 10-15 lb. The white tail is not absolutely constant, some individuals having blackish tails.

Distribution.—The White-tailed Mongoose is common in all the National Parks and National Reserves of Kenya, and is widely distributed, in various local races, throughout Africa.

Habits.—Strictly nocturnal, and solitary in habit, this large Mongoose may not uncommonly be noticed moving about at sundown and after, a fine specimen was seen in the Nairobi National Park at dusk. It carries its head and tail low as it trots along, and the whiteness of the tail readily catches the eye. It preys upon birds up to the size of guineafowl (is a bold poultry thief), small mammals,

167

MARSH, OR WATER MONGOOSE

and rodents, hares, cane rats, insects and grubs, frogs, lizards and eggs; and also attacks and kills snakes. Heller found a small cobra in the stomach of one in Kenya. It is a lover of fairly dense bush or undergrowth, and is rarely found far from such surroundings. When attacked by dogs it fights pluckily, exuding a powerful musky odour from its scent glands. It occasionally utters a cackling sort of bark. Two are usually born in a litter : in a hole or rock crevice.

RIVER, OR MARSH MONGOOSE

Atilax paludinosus rubescens (Hollister)

Field Impression.—A large, long-haired, wholly dark brown Mongoose, looking black at a distance, always seen near rivers or marshy surroundings.

Descriptive Notes.—This Mongoose is easily identified on account of its fairly large size and rather robust form and prevalent dark brown colouration. The coat is long and shaggy, and the long tail—shaggy at base—becomes more pointed at tip. Head broad and rather blunt at muzzle, and ears short and rounded. Length of body about 24 inches, and tail another 13-14 inches. The body hairs are ringed with blackish or dark brown and pale yellow but the limbs are darker with wholly dark brown hairs.

Distribution.—This Mongoose is more or less entirely confined to marshy areas, or the close neighbourhood of streams or rivers. It has definitely been recorded from Mara N.R. But it is likely to occur in suitable surroundings anywhere. Being nocturnal, it is not often seen except by chance.

Habits.—As it usually dwells in thick herbage, reeds, and so on, near water, it is not easy to see as a rule. Sometimes, however, one sees this Mongoose moving about, or crossing a road, in such localities, and its widely splayed toe prints are quite often seen in the mud, together with the mashed up remains of crabs which it frequently devours. It is

BANDED MONGOOSE

BLACK-TIPPED MONGOOSE

DWARF MONGOOSE

fairly solitary, and mostly observed in pairs or family parties of three or four, or singly. It preys on birds which roost or nest in such localities, small rodents, frogs, crabs, and insects of various sorts as well as (probably) snakes and other reptiles. Its long-haired coat, and dark colouring tend to make it look larger than it really is when seen indistinctly in dense herbage. I have heard them utter a high-pitched cough, or bark. Like the White-tailed Mongoose, the River Mongoose sometimes attacks poultry if the latter are left out near its habitat.

BANDED MONGOOSE

Mungos mungo colonus (Heller)

Field Impression.—Usually seen in troops. Dark brown or grey, with conspicuous, transverse darker bands along body behind shoulders, becoming more distinct towards tail. Coat fairly coarse, and tail tapering, darker at tip.

Descriptive Notes.—Grizzled grey, banded on the hinder portion of the body with a blending of dirty whitish, through reddish to black transverse stripes. The tail, about 8 inches long, is coarsely haired at base becoming scantily so at tip, which is blackish. Body hairs coarse and wiry. Length of head and body about 16 inches.

Distribution.—Apparently not recorded from Nairobi National Park. Quite common in Tsavo National Park East. They are recorded as common in Amboseli and Mara National Reserves, but not listed from Marsabit. In bush country this is a widely distributed Mongoose, generally speaking.

Habits.—The Banded Mongoose is a sociable, diurnal species which is almost certain to be seen sooner or later in areas in which it occurs. It moves about in considerable troops which, usually consist of from half a dozen to fifteen or more individuals, but sometimes aggregate as many as thirty. When crossing an open space (such as a road) the members of such a troop follow one another closely, producing an almost "rope"-like effect at a distance.

Individuals of all ages and sizes comprise such a pack. As they run about quartering the veld for insects, grubs, snails, the eggs of locusts, and so on, these Mongooses utter low-pitched chattering cries, varied with whistling notes, which may be heard from some distance. They also growl, and make slight barking sounds, when angry. They are usually found in the neighbourhood of termite hills, in holes in which they take refuge when alarmed. In addition to insects and grubs, these Mongooses feed on mice, small reptiles, eggs and young of small ground-nesting birds, and wild fruits and berries. This Mongoose is principally insectivorous, and a highly useful mammal. It tames easily.

BLACK-TIPPED MONGOOSE

Herpestes sanguineus ibeae (Wroughton)

Field Impression.—A very slender, stoat-like little animal, grizzled rufous-brown in colour, with a long black-tipped tail—the latter usually curled upwards at the tip. Frequently seen scampering across the road.

Descriptive Notes.—About 15 inches long in body, with tail of equal length, this Mongoose is the most commonly seen one in Kenya. Its rather grizzled, or speckled coat of wiry, fine hairs, is brown strongly tinged with rufous, and the very long, tapering tail has a pronounced black tip. Face pointed, and ears very narrow and short.

Distribution.—More or less common everywhere.

Habits.—The Black-tipped Mongoose is also known as the Slender Mongoose. It is more or less diurnal, and can often be observed darting across a road, usually whisking its tail high in the air in a semi-defiant manner. When trotting along at its normal pace it carries the long tail straight out behind, with the tip gracefully upcurled. It is solitary in disposition, seldom more than a pair being seen together, and it is usually encountered alone.

The black-tipped Mongoose preys on snakes and lizards, small rodents, birds and birds' eggs, insects and grubs of many kinds, and wild fruits. All these smaller Carnivora are of great assitance to man in combatting Bubonic plague by preying very largely on the mice and gerbilles which are the chief carriers of this terrible disease. Unfortunately they are also very prone to Rabies. The Black-tipped Mongoose is a bad egg thief, and also attacks unguarded chicks—but the good it does in destroying snakes and small rodents probably far outweighs occasional harm. It can easily be tamed, and makes an intelligent and attractive pet. The young are born in rock-crevices, holes, or hollows in trees or stumps.

DWARF MONGOOSE

Helogale undulata rufula (Thomas)

(Swahili : *Kitafe*)

Field Impression.—A very small, rather short-tailed, Mongoose, plain grey-brown in colour, which associates in small troops; and which is usually seen in the neighbourhood of rocks or antheaps in bushy country.

Descriptive Notes.—The smallest of the Mongooses, body and head only measuring about 8-9 inches, with another 5 inches or so of tail. They vary from a dark, grizzly grey-brown to dark brownish-slate, the hairs being "ticked" with paler colour. Usually slightly more rufous tinted round head and chest. In some of the coastal areas almost black specimens are seen. On account of the noticeably proportionately short tail, this species is sometimes called the Short-tailed Mongoose—but "Dwarf" or "Pigmy" are more descriptive.

Distribution.—Not recorded yet from Nairobi National Park, but plentiful at Amboseli, Mara, and Marsabit National Reserves, and we saw one troop in Western Tsavo National Park (not counting the delightful tame one owned by Mr. and Mrs. C. W. Marshall!). Generally plentiful in most thorny scrub or bush areas. They occur also in Tsavo National Park (East).

Habits.—Like the Banded Mongoose, these dwarf Mongooses associate in troops, though usually smaller in size than those of the former. They are usually plentiful wherever there are large white ant hills or mounds, in holes of which they breed and take refuge. They also breed in the hollows of trees, which they stuff with grass.

Dwarf Mongooses are active little creatures, always keenly bustling about after insects, grubs, berries, birds'

ZORILLA

eggs, small reptiles, and so on. During these forays, which are accompanied by much scuffling of dried leaves and scratching about, they utter bird-like whistles and chirping notes : but they growl, and utter miniature barking sounds, when annoyed or suspicious. They are said to unite to attack and kill snakes. Dwarf Mongooses make the most delightful, intelligent and affectionate pets. The young are little larger than mice, and 2-4 in a litter.

There are 4 species of Dwarf Mongoose in Kenya.

ZORILLA

Ictonyx striatus albescens (Heller)

(Kiswahili : *Kicheche*)

Field Impression.—Somewhat mongoose-like in form, but richly striped in black and white along the back, rather like a skunk. Tail long and bushy, also balck and white.

Descriptive Notes.—Length of head and body about 12 inches, with another 9 inches of tail. Back white, with a longitudinal black stripe along the middle of back, and another a little lower down on either side of it. Face black, with a white patch in front of each ear and a white spot between the eyes. Tail white marked with black, the hair long and coarse. Underparts and short legs black. Coat, particularly along the back, fairly long and coarse, Young marked similarly to adults, but with shorter fur.

Distribution.—Common in all National Parks and Reserves, and recorded up to 12,000 feet in Mount Kenya National Park.

Habits.—The Zorilla (or Cape Polecat, as it was formerly called) is a strictly nocturnal creature, and consequently though it may be plentiful in an area it is very seldom seen—except sometimes in the glare of a car's headlights by night. It occurs in all types of country and is widely distributed throughout Africa. It usually trots along with the back slightly hunched, but when angry or excited the long dorsal hairs are erected, and the tail raised and curled

175

forward over the back, and at such times it utters a series of high-pitched screams. Its chief method of defence is to eject a powerful and unpleasant scent from its anal glands— somewhat after the manner of a skunk—and anything affected by this (such as an attacking dog) will bear the scent for several days.

The Zorilla is solitary in disposition, and by day shelters in rock crevices or burrows. According to Shortridge, Zorillas are more essentially carnivorous than Mongooses, preying very largely on small field rodents which they spend much time in digging out. They are inveterate snake killers, and also prey on hares, cane rats, birds (from guineafowl down), frogs, eggs, locusts and insects. They can be bad poultry killers; 1—3 young are born in a litter.

RATEL, OR HONEY BADGER

Mellivora capensis sagulata (Hollister)

(Kiswahili : *Nyegere*)

Field Impression.—A badger-like animal with hardly visible ears : grey above, black below—with a white area on crown dividing grey of back from black of underparts. Tail short and bushy.

Descriptive Notes.—Total length about 2¾ feet. The Ratel is a heavily-built creature, like a badger, with plantigrade feet and bear-like stout digging claws. It is clad in short, coarse fur : dark grey on the back, white on top of head and flanks, and dark brown or black on limbs and underparts. The head is bluntly pointed, with very small eyes and barely visible ears. The short bushy tail has a dark tip. Young ones are coloured rusty-brown above, with no paler dividing line.

Distribution.—The Ratel occurs in most of the Kenya National Parks and Reserves, but is not common, and being nocturnal is not very often seen—except at dawn or dusk or after dark.

Habits.—This is one of the most courageous and admirable little beasts in Africa. Normally inoffensive and peacefully inclined, it will attack at once if interfered with—no matter what the odds. Having a singularly tough and elastic skin it will stand the severest mauling from several dogs without apparent harm, but will usually inflict such punishment on its adversaries that it frequently wins the day. Like the European badger, once it gets a tooth-hold, the Ratel hangs on till the bitter end and nothing, short of death, will usually dislodge it!

Ratels of course prey very largely on the grubs of wild bees, when the hives can be dug out from hollows in the ground or tree roots. The Honey Guide (*Indicator*) will often lead ratels to such hives—the two working in co-

CLAWLESS OTTER

operation : the bird being keenest on the wax of the combs, the Ratel devouring grubs and honey. Its tough skin is apparently impervious to bee-stings. In addition to honey and bee grubs, Ratels prey on small mammals, young birds and eggs, insects, grubs, reptiles, tortoises, wild fruits, berries and roots. It is a famed killer of snakes. It is a powerful digger. About 2 young are born; in a rock-crevice or underground.

CLAWLESS OTTER

Aonyx capensis helios (Heller)

(Kiswahili : *Fisi maji*)

Field Impression.—Pale reddish-brown above, with white chin and throat. Very short legged, and with very short round ears. Tail ("rudder") long, somewhat flattened, and tapering to a point. Usually seen during the day in the water, or very near it.

Descriptive Notes.—The head of the Otter is rather rounded, with very long whiskers. The toes of the hind feet are webbed, and there are no claws on the forefeet, and only two small nails on the hind ones.

The ears are very small, and the colour ranges from dark to pale reddish-brown, with upper lips, cheeks, chin and throat white. Total length about 5 feet, of which the tail measures about 2 feet. Weight up to about 40 lb. as a rule, but records up to 63 lb. have been killed in Natal.

Distribution.—Rare in Nairobi National Park, but common at Amboseli and Mara. Otters can be expected to exist anywhere along rivers, streams or large dams.

Habits.—It is always a matter of luck to catch a glimpse of an Otter during the day. On the other hand they are not entirely nocturnal, and in undisturbed areas may sometimes be noticed swimming, or playing on the bank or rocks, during the day. They are usually seen singly or in pairs, but sometimes family parties of several individuals may be seen hunting or playing together. They favour specially

AARD-WOLF

WITH "CAPE" RAISED

selected pools where they may be encountered quite often, or at least their tracks regularly seen. Besides fish, Otters prey largely on crabs, aquatic waterfowl, and freshwater mussels, in addition to frogs and any small creatures which they can overpower up to the size of cane rats on land. Aquatic food is brought ashore to eat, as is indicated by the litter of crab shells, scales, etc., often seen on rocks near the water. Two to three cubs are born in a litter, and these have to be taught to take to the water by the parents. The young are usually born in holes in dense vegetation near the water, or hollows between overhanging tree roots, etc.

AARD WOLF

Proteles cristatus termes (Heller)

(Kiswahili : *Fisi ndogo*)

Field Impression.—It resembles a small, very lightly built striped hyena—about as big as a jackal.

Descriptive Notes.—The Aard Wolf is a pale sandy-rufous in ground colour, marked with a few conspicuous vertical brown stripes on the sides, with horizontal bands on the upper parts of the limbs, and conspicuous longitudinal bands across the chest. There is a heavy mane of long hairs (buff with black tips) along the back which is erected under excitement; and the bushy tail is longer than that of a hyena, and black along the terminal half. Ears narrow, fairly long and pointed. Front of face black. Shoulder height 18—20 inches. Length, from tip of nose to root of tail, about 3 feet.

Distribution.—The Aard Wolf occurs in Nairobi National Park but is rarely seen during the day. The same applies to Tsavo National Park, where it is recorded as common in the western area, but rarely seen. It is listed in the Marsabit area.

Habits.—The Aard Wolf is an inhabitant of scrubby bush country or open sand-plains, and is not found in forest areas. During the day it usually lies up in underground burrows, several individuals often occupying one earth. I have twice seen an Aard Wolf abroad in daylight, on both occasions fairly late in the afternoon, and as they are very timid, shy creatures one seldom obtains much more than a glimpse of them. Their teeth are exceedingly small and weak, and they live almost entirely on insects, white ants, beetles, etc., though they are stated to take eggs and young of ground-nesting birds as well. Where it occurs, it is sometimes locally called a "striped hyena", which is misleading!

The Aard Wolf is a very useful mammal, and there is no doubt that it devours considerable numbers of termites, and also small rodents such as gerbilles which transmit Bubonic Plague. When attacked by dogs, it emits a vile smelling liquid from its anal glands. Two to four young are reared in a burrow.

SILVER-BACKED JACKAL

Canis mesomelas elgonae (Heller)

(Kiswahili : *Bweha*)

Field Impression.—The common jackal of the plains and fairly open savanna bush. The dark back, stippled with silvery grey hairs, forms a saddle in marked contrast with the yellowish-rufous flanks and legs. Brush only moderately bushy, with usually a darker tip. Ears rather long and pointed, and head rather fox-like.

Descriptive Notes.—Rather larger than a European fox, and decidedly higher on the leg, the jackal is a true dog, and by some authorities is considered to be the ancestor of our domestic breeds. It has five toes on the front foot, and four on the hind one. Upper part of head greyish, muzzle and cheeks more sandy—as are the backs of the large pointed ears and the outer sides of the limbs. Abdomen, and inner sides of legs, paling almost to white. Tail moderately bushy, marked with darker hairs and usually with a dark tip. Eyes very keen in expression, yellowish in colour. The back is

THE JACKALS

BLACK-BACKED JACKAL

SILVER JACKAL

SIDE-STRIPED OR
GREY JACKAL

marked with a pronounced "saddle" of white-tipped and black hairs, imparting a silvery appearance at a distance—not quite so richly marked as in the typical *C. Mesomelas*, or Black-backed Jackal; a variety of which (*C. Mesomelas mcmillani* Heller) occurs in the Tsavo area. Length of head and body about 3—3½ feet. Tail 13—14 inches. Weight averages about 21 lb.

Distribution.—Plentiful in Nairobi National Park : Tsavo National Park : Amboseli, N.R., and Marsabit, N.R. Jackals are not usually found in mountain forest country.

Habits.—Jackals are usually seen in pairs, threes or fours, or solitary, though considerable numbers will gather at a place where lions have killed, to wait about patiently for any left-over scraps. They are mainly scavengers, but also hunt small mammals, reptiles and insects, game birds and others whose young and eggs are incubated on the ground : as well as the young of antelopes if these can be snatched while temporarily unguarded. In this connection, a pair of jackals have been seen taking it in turns to try to lure a female wildebeest into charging one of them, while the other planned to attack the newly-born youngster. Jackals also eat bush fruits and berries in season, and have been known to prey on the eggs and young of ostriches when the opportunity is afforded.

The Silver-backed jackal is mainly nocturnal, but is not uncommonly observed trotting about by day, especially when lions or other carnivora have killed in the neighbourhood. During the day these jackals couch mainly in the grass, or under bushes, and very often the pointed tips of their ears sticking up above the grass are the first objects to catch the attention. A jackal trots with his head usually slightly lower than the line of the shoulders, and the brush extended horizontally, tip drooping downwards.

At night, or shortly after dusk, he usually utters an abrupt yell, followed closely by three or four shorter notes, sounding something like : *Bweha! bwe-bwe-bwe-bwe!* Hence the Swahili name "*Bweha*". When very excited, as when lions have just pulled down some quarry, jackals peal out into a thrillingly wild wailing chorus, which quavers fiercely in the night air—a sort of long-drawn *EEEeeeaa-ouww*, always a fascinating sound to those who love the

184

African wilderness. They also utter an abrupt "kek-kek" note on occasions, often a warning that large carnivora are on the move.

The 3—4 cubs are born in holes or crevices between rocks : both parents assist to forage for them, and, when very young, food is regurgitated for them. I have watched as many as 20—30 jackals feeding on the remains of a lion's kill, their tails all waving high in the air with pleasure!

GREY or SIDE-STRIPED JACKAL

Canis adustus notatus (Heller)

(Kiswahili : *Bweha*)

Field Impression.—Rather higher on the leg than the Silver-backed Jackal, drab browny-grey all over with no well-marked "saddle", with shorter ears and a fuller, darker brush—usually with a white tip. Much more nocturnal, and far more rarely seen, than the Silver-backed Jackal, and prefers more wooded or densely bushed country.

Descriptive Notes.—This jackal stands rather higher at the shoulder than the previous species, and its shorter ears and generally greyer colouring gives it a rather more wolf-like aspect. Although the back is rather darker than the rest of the body, there is no clear cut distinction line. But along each side of the body there is a more or less distinct whitish stripe, hardly visible in some specimens. The muzzle (which is rather broader than that of the Silver-back), chest, and limbs are more or less tan-coloured, and the tail, which is much more bushy than that of the other type, is usually darker than the rest of the body—sometimes more or less black—with usually a pronounced white tip. Some individuals, however, lack the white tag to the brush. Length from nose to root of tail about 28 inches. Length of tail about 10 inches. Males probably weigh up to 30 lb.

Distribution.—Grey Jackals are rare in Nairobi National Park and Amboseli, but are common in Mara National Reserve. They are not recorded from Tsavo National Park, but occur in the Marsabit area.

Habits.—This is a rather heavier, thicker-coated species than the Silver-backed Jackal, and very much more solitary and nocturnal. Hence it may be present in an area some time before it is recorded. It seems to prefer rather denser bush surroundings and is more sluggish in disposition. It is also far less noisy at night, and its call is lower in tone, and usually consists of a long-drawn note followed by three or four single barks, uttered in slower succession than the rapidly uttered call of the common jackal.

The Grey Jackal sometimes interbreeds with domestic dogs, according to A. Blayney Percival.

BAT-EARED FOX

Otocyon megalotis virgatus (Miller)

(Kiswahili : *Bweha masigio*)

Field Impression.—Its relatively enormous ears, greyish drab colouring, black face, legs, and tip of brush, as well as its small size, should easily distinguish this little fox.

Descriptive Notes.—Greyish-brown above, tinged with rufous-ochre on upper part of brush and flanks, and paler below, the Bat-eared Fox has a black face and limbs (which are short), and black on the top and tip of its bushy tail. Its ears are enormously large and more or less oval shaped, black-tipped and rufous bases behind, and white fringed in front. Length about 2 feet. Tail 1 foot. Weight 6—8½ lb. Pupil of eye vertical, like those of all foxes.

Distribution.—Fairly common in Nairobi National Park, Tsavo National Park, Amboseli National Reserve, and Marsabit National Reserve. Not recorded from Mara.

Habits.—This most attractive little fox can quite easily be seen in the Nairobi National Park towards sundown, or in the very early mornings, as, though nocturnal, family parties appear at those times to lie about near the entrances of their burrows, where they spend most of the daylight hours. When alarmed, they crouch down, depressing their long ears flat on either side.

BAT-EARED FOX

They are principally insectivorous, but catch small rodents such as mice and gerbilles, and eat the nestlings and eggs of ground-nesting birds, as well as wild fruits, lizards, tuberous roots, etc. A captive pair used to utter growls when quarrelling over food, but their usual note seemed to be a rather melancholy, long-drawn but not unmusical whine. This species is also known as Delalande's Fox. As a whole, these little foxes favour rather open sandy country.

Three to five cubs are born in a burrow. Apparently these small foxes are frequently caught by the larger birds of prey.

PRIMATES

(Monkeys and Baboons and Galagos)

Kenya contains many beautiful species of monkeys. In this work, however, I must confine myself to those most likely to be seen in the National Parks or National Reserves.

BABOONS

There are two well-defined species of Baboon to be seen in the areas indicated. These are :—

1. NEUMANN'S OLIVE BABOON

Papio anubis neumanni (Matschie)

(Kiswahili : *Nyani* (for all Baboons))

Field Impression.—A very heavily-built baboon, with bushy hair on cheeks; and hairy, bushy mane developed on shoulders—especially in large males. Generally of a speckled grey-brown colour, with pink bare patch below tail. Muzzle long and dog-like. Tail comparatively short, and held in a loop : basal third upright and latter portion hanging down. Length of head and body about 3 feet. Tail about 1½ feet. This is the common species in the Nairobi National Park.

2. YELLOW BABOON

Papio cynocephalus cynocephalus Linnaeus.

Field Impression.—A longer legged, lighter built animal. Hair on cheeks not bushy, and that on shoulders not form-

THE BABOONS

NEUMANN'S OLIVE BABOON

YELLOW BABOON

ing a thick mane. Olive brown in colour, paler below and on cheeks. Face dark, and muzzle shorter than in Neumann's Baboon. Size about the same, though possibly higher at the shoulder. Tail slightly longer. This species is common at Amboseli and Tsavo.

Habits (*generally*).—The above notes on distribution are incomplete, and only apply to my own observations. The two species are sufficiently distinct in appearance to make identification easy if one remembers that Neumann's Olive Baboon is thickset, shaggy coated, with a thick mane on shoulders and round cheeks, and olive grey all over : whereas the Yellow Baboon is more slender in form, olive brown above and paler below and on cheeks, with comparatively short fur and no pronounced mane on cheeks and shoulders.

I found Neumann's Baboon common in the Moiben area near Eldoret, and it was the only species seen in Nairobi National Park. In habits, both species of Baboon are fairly similar. They are large, powerful monkeys with characteristic, more or less pointed "dog-like" faces, spending more time patrolling the ground for their food than in the trees, to which they as a rule resort only for sleeping purposes or as look-out posts. They occur frequently in rocky, or mountainous localities; and they can move with ease along the steepest rock faces, and take refuge in crevices and caves. An ordinary monkey usually takes to the trees for refuge : Baboons, in a tree, usually descend or jump down and make away over the ground when approached.

Baboons are highly intelligent and extremely watchful. Although their powers of scent are little better than those of humans, their eyesight is extremely good, and they can usually discern a human form—or that of a carnivorous animal—even if the intruder remains perfectly still. For this reason their vigilance at waterholes is greatly respected by other animals which cannot identify stationary forms if not assisted by the wind. They wander about the veld in large troops, usually dominated by a large and very powerful senior male, searching for roots and wild fruits, insects, grubs, spiders, eggs, and even scorpions—from which they deftly first snatch the stinging tail. They possess most formidable teeth—those of a big male almost

191

as large as those of a leopard—and can be most powerful and dangerous antagonists as they are very strong. When grappling with a dog, a Baboon seizes him with all four limbs : pushing the body away while he tears out a huge chunk of flesh, and many a large dog has been fatally injured by this method of attack.

The leopard is the Baboon's chief natural enemy, and it is regarded with such dread by Baboons that the mere sight of one will cause an hysterical, threatening outcry of raucous barks, shouts and screams. The leopard usually approaches Baboons in stealth; rushes in and grabs one quickly, and then either springs away with it into some inaccessible place, or else leaves it until all the hubbub has died down and the rest of the troop has fled, before returning to eat it. If he is too late in getting out of the way, even a leopard may be torn to pieces by the infuriated mob! Nonetheless, the leopard probably destroys numerous Baboons; and in areas where "Spots" has been exterminated completely, Baboons rapidly become a serious menace to cultivated crops, etc.

Baboons are always interesting to watch, and their antics and intelligent behaviour, and the ease with which they respond to being fed from cars, etc., form a great temptation to visitors to National Parks in Africa to encourage such familiarity. This should never be done, however, because, with the Baboon, familiarity rapidly breeds contempt! In a short while they begin to climb on to a car to seek titbits, and a hasty push or slap from an unwilling visitor (especially from a child) may well prompt a ferocious attack which spells disaster for all concerned. It cannot be sufficiently emphasised that adult Baboons are moody and unpredictable in temper, and inclined to become treacherous if thwarted or suddenly alarmed.

The normal call of the Baboon is a loud, challenging bark or grunt, but they utter a variety of softer "conversational" notes or chattering sounds, and when frightened or caught they utter piercing screams. Usually one infant is born at a time, at any time of the year, and female Baboons treat all baby ones with great affection, frequently fondling infants other than their own. The baby is at first carried under its mother's chest, where it clings to the long hair; but as it gets older it frequently rides, jockey-like, on its mother's back. The big males are great disciplinarians, dealing out chastisement to all and sundry when they consider it due.

Baboons, of one species or another, occur everywhere except in dense forest areas.

BLACK-FACED GUENON, OR VERVET MONKEY

Cercopithecus aethiops johnstoni (Pocock)

(Kiswahili : *Tumbili*)

Field Impression.—Small grey Monkeys with conspicuous black faces and long, black-tipped tails. White cheek tufts, and white below. The commonest East African Monkey generally.

Descriptive Notes.—The Vervet is easily distinguished on account of its grey colouring and pronounced black face with white cheek tufts. Its coat varies locally in greenish or yellowish tinge, but is always more or less grey above and white below. Tail long and slender, with black tip. The scrotum of the male is bright blue, and there is a rufous patch at the base of the tail. There is a more or less distinct white bar across the bushy eyebrows. Limbs black. Newly-born young have flesh-coloured faces. Total length about $4\frac{1}{2}$ feet, of which the tail measures 2 feet. Weight about 5 lbs. (Percival).

Distribution.—The Vervet is common in all the Kenya National Parks and National Reserves, though it is not a forest Monkey. It is usually found in the fairly dense belts bordering streams or rivers, but may be met with anywhere among fairly large trees or clumps of bush.

Habits.—Vervets are very gregarious, associating in troops from about 20 or 30 to much larger numbers. They are active, cunning and inquisitive, and fearfully destructive to all agricultural produce—particularly fruit and maize. Anyone who wants to test their smartness at pilfering need only picnic at Mzima Springs, in Western Tsavo Park, where vervets will surround him in no time, and cunningly

VERVET MONKEY

snatch items out of his luncheon basket from behind his back! They are attractive, highly entertaining little creatures which rapidly become very tame with the least encouragement, but unfortunately become bold thieves.

Their principal enemies are the larger eagles (particularly the great Crowned Eagle) and leopards. The sight of either of these dreaded foes results in an outburst of chattering, raucous coughs (which sound rather like "*Jokko-jokko-jokko-jokko*") followed by chickering notes : an alarm which is taken up at once by other troops in the neighbourhood. From the trees overhead they will follow a leopard as he moves along the ground, mobbing him loudly as long as he keeps in sight, and should a troop of Vervets be seen acting thus it is always worth while to wait in case one should catch a glimpse of a leopard. In the same way, the sight of many vultures waiting patiently in the trees round a certain area often reveals the presence of lions on a kill. Leopards will co-operate cleverly to catch a Vervet : one boldly walking along in plain view, or sunning himself deliberately to attract the attention of the Monkeys, while his mate waits concealed along a leaf-covered bough to snatch one of the unsuspecting, excited mob!

Vervets prey on insects, spiders, grubs, fruits of all kinds, leaves and seeds of various trees, including the wild lettuce, the young and eggs of birds (of which they are fearfully destructive), and they are particularly fond of the gum which exudes from various species of Acacia. The newly born infants cling to their mothers' breasts, or sprawl across their backs—their tail-tips usually curled round the tails of their mothers. The female Vervet is very devoted to all baby Monkeys, and will fondle and caress those of her neighbours. I have had personal experience of at least one case when an entirely strange, captive baby Monkey was taken away and apparently cherished by a female of another wild troop. Breeding takes place throughout the year, and the younger animals of a troop keep very much to their "Age Groups" Old males sometimes occur solitarily, and then become bold thieves of domestic fruit and poultry eggs.

BLUE MONKEY

SYKES MONKEY

TYPICAL
ATTITUDES
OF
BLUE MONKEY

1. BLUE MONKEY

Cercopithecus mitis neumanni (Matschie)

2. SYKE'S MONKEY

Cercopithecus mitis kolbi (Neumann)

(Kiswahili : *Kima*)

Field Impression.—Both these closely related monkeys are very similar in general proportions and colouration, but Syke's Monkey has a pronounced white gorget round its throat and the sides of its neck, and is slightly rufous on the rump. Otherwise, they are both rather thickset monkeys, generally dark grey, blacker below and on limbs, with a black band across the forehead. Cheeks very full, greyish, and no white fringe. Long tail usually carried somewhat like that of a baboon, upright and then downwards in a loop. Fur fairly long and soft and beautiful.

Descriptive Notes.—The two species can be distinguished as above. The Blue Monkey has no white throat or neck gorget, and is generally grey, with a slight silvery tinge owing to the speckled hairs above, and the darker or black colouring below and on the limbs. There is a pale fringe (not white) along the eyebrows, superseded by a black head patch, and the throat is paler. The grey of the well haired cheeks and the darker centre of the face are barely distinguishable, giving quite a different expression from that of the richly contrasted face of the Vervet. It is a slightly larger, more robust-looking Monkey owing to its thicker coat, and at a distance (especially in the shade of its forest habitat) looks black.

Distribution.—Only in forest, or forest patches. Rare in Nairobi National Park. Common in parts of Tsavo National Park, and in Marsabit National Reserve. Neither occur at Amboseli, but the Blue is recorded from Mara. One or other or both probably occur in the Mountain Forest National Parks.

Habits.—These "Blue" Monkeys are essentially forest dwellers. I was able to make a few observations on the Blue Monkey along the Tangaseer and Moiben rivers on the Kapsiliat Estate, and noted that it was rarely seen away from the large tress and gallery forest fringing these streams. Here it occurred in small troops, but was very much shyer than the Vervet. The beautiful Colobus Monkeys also inhabited these streamside forest galleries.

When gazing quietly at you, half-concealed among the foliage, the Blue Monkey has a characteristic habit of looping its tail loosely round a branch. When walking, either along a branch or on the ground, it invariably carries its tail in a bold vertical loop—the tip hanging down and slightly inclined inwards.

Sounds definitely associated with the Blue Monkey were a whistling chatter, and a call sounding like "*nyah*". Another call was a soft, almost cricket-like "*tick*," which was uttered from time to time.

Blayney Percival records that Blue Monkeys used to form the staple food of the Wandorobo of the Mau forests. Moreover, at one time the traders offered such high prices for the beautiful fur, that the tribesmen killed the monkeys in great numbers. The result was near-extermination for the species.

The food seems to consist mainly of leaves and vegetable matter, and neither the Syke's nor the Blue Monkeys are quite so destructive to crops as the Vervet : both of the former being shyer and less venturesome species.

COPPER-TAILED WHITE-NOSED MONKEY

Cercopithecus nictitans schmidti (Matschie)

Field Impression.—This is a forest-dwelling Monkey of small medium size (about as large as a Vervet), olive brown in colour above, white below. It has a very long and slender tail, bright coppery-red on the lower part. It has white cheeks and a very conspicuous white nose—like a blob of white putty!

Descriptive Notes.—The limbs are darker brown, and the bare skin round the eyes is bright blue.

Distribution.—Mainly Uganda and Belgian Congo and parts of Western Kenya, but always in forested areas. It

is recorded as common in the Mara National Reserve, but in no other of the Kenya National Parks or National Reserves.

Habits.—I have not seen this attractive little Monkey in its wild state, and the accompanying sketches and description were taken from a pair in captivity at the Ruwenzori Hotel, Mutwanga, in the Congo. It is said to betray its presence in the forest habitat which it favours by its whistling, chirruping call. The head is very rounded over the forehead and rather flat on top; and as it walks or runs the hindquarters appear higher than the forequarters, and the long tail is carried downwards and outwards. The blue skin round the eyes, and the startling white nose patch, impart a most odd expression to its face! It may be seen in the Maramagamba forest of the Queen Elizabeth National Park of Uganda.

BLACK-AND-WHITE COLOBUS

Colobus polykomos

(Kiswahili : *Mbega*)

Field Impression.—A fairly large, very handsome Monkey coloured black and white in contrasting manner. Black, with flowing white mantle along sides and rump, with long white bushy tail. Forehead band, cheeks, and beard white. Newly-born juvenile pure white. Only found in forest, or forest patches.

Descriptive Notes.—The Colobus Monkeys comprise a group of which the principal character is that the thumb is lacking. The Black and White Colobus is the most beautiful of the Kenya Monkeys, and is restricted to true forest, and forest patches or galleries in the higher levels. It is pitch black above, with long, sweeping white hairs forming a silky white mantle along the sides and lower back. Forehead band, cheeks and shaggy short beard on chin are also white; while the long tail is clothed with bushy white hairs. Length of head and body about 32 inches, while the tail measures about 40 inches. The newly born young are white.

Distribution.—The Colobus may be seen in the Mountain Forest National Parks of Mount Kenya and the Aberdares, also at Mara. It is a strictly forest-dwelling species, of the higher altitudes.

Habits.—The Black-and-White Colobus (also known as the Guereza) haunts the taller trees of the dense forests, or the galleries bordering mountain streams, where its long white mantle and bushy white tail harmonise wonderfully with the tufts and beards of light-coloured lichens which frequently adorn the twigs and branches of such trees. To see a troop of them leaping gracefully from branch to branch, their long mantles flowing behind them, is a wonderful and fascinating sight. They live almost entirely upon various forest leaves and vegetable matter and are as harmless as they are beautiful. They rarely leave the trees, obtaining water from hollows in the trunks or branches, and feed mainly in the early mornings and evenings. At dawn their curious throbbing or rolling croaking chorus may be heard swelling in concert through the mist-girt forests. Colobus are rather solemn and serious in disposition, and are rarely seen gambolling about like vervets and other monkeys. I have heard them utter shrill whistling cries—which probably come from younger ones—but normally, apart from the above-described morning chorus, they are silent, and may well be overlooked by the casual visitor to their haunts. As they quietly watch the intruder, from their concealment among the foliage, the long pendant white tails can easily be mistaken for the surrounding beard-like lichens : and probably the first indication of their presence may be announced by the crashing sounds which accompany their departure through the treetops.

THE GALAGOS

1. BUSH BABY

Galago crassicaudatus

Descriptive Notes.—About as large as a small monkey, but with more pointed face and large oval-shaped ears. Its

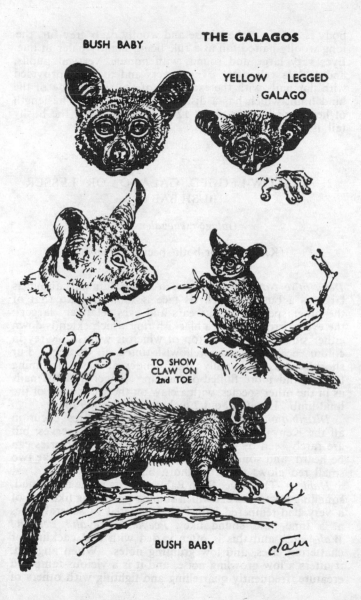

THE GALAGOS

BUSH BABY

YELLOW LEGGED GALAGO

TO SHOW CLAW ON 2nd TOE

BUSH BABY

203

body is clad in rather dense and woolly drab grey fur, the long woolly-haired tail as a rule being slightly paler in hue. Eyes very large and round, with minute, vertical pupils, and eyelids yellowish. The fingers and toes are provided with flat nails with the exception of the second toe of the hind limb, which has a distinct claw instead. The length of head and body is about 12—14 inches, while the bushy tail is about a foot long.

2. YELLOW-LEGGED GALAGO, OR LESSER BUSH BABY

Galago senegalensis.

(Kiswahili for both species : *komba.*)

Descriptive Notes.—A very much smaller animal, about as large as a bush squirrel. Its face is rounder than that of the other species, and its ears and eyes relatively larger : the eyes surrounded by a blackish ring which extends down either side of snout, the top of which is whitish. Grey in colour, becoming more yellowish-tinted on the legs. Fur short, close and woolly : tail slender at base, becoming thicker and more fluffed-out at tip. Finger and toe nails as in the other species, with a claw on the second toe of the hind limb. Length about 7 inches : tail about 9 inches.

Distribution.—These very nocturnal creatures occur in all the Kenya National Parks and National Reserves, but are rarely seen by day. At night, however, their cries can be heard, and sometimes their eyes reflect the light like two small red glows from the thorn bushes.

Habits.—The larger Bush Baby owes its name to its loud, squalling nocturnal cry which sounds something like that of a very bad-tempered baby! It is uttered in several notes at a time, and sound like : *Peeyah! Peeyah! Peeyah! Wah-wah!*, and this is often varied with odd cackling or chattering cries, and low grunting notes. When angered, it utters a low growling noise, and it is a vicious-tempered creature, frequently quarrelling and fighting with others of its kind. It preys upon roosting birds and their eggs, insects of all kinds, and wild fruits and berries. During the day it sleeps curled up snugly in a tree hollow, or very often among masses of twined creepers which festoon the branches of trees or shrubs, coming out at dusk to prowl stealthily about among the branches, but quite often moving about on the ground—when it often carries its tail erect, like that of a cat. Although most at home in the trees, it is not so active, nor can it make such amazing leaps, as its smaller relative. Both species of Galago are closely related to the Lemurs of Madagascar. Usually one offspring is born at a time, but occasionally two, and the young cling to the mother's fur. They are usually born in hollows of trees. Like the Vervet, the Galago is extremely fond of the Acacia Gum. This species is extremely noisy at night, and where plentiful its screaming calls can often be heard, as individuals reply to each other.

The smaller *Yellow-legged Galago* occurs usually in country where there are thorn trees, but frequently the two species are found together. This is a far more active little creature, thoroughly sprite-like in habits as well as appearance. It proceeds in a series of rapid hops, and can take the most astonishing jumps from one place to another, but rarely leaves the security of the trees. Its call is quite different—being a rapidly uttered : *myah-myah-myah-myah*. It also utters whistling notes at times. It preys on insects, berries, wild fruits, eggs and nestlings, and Acacia Gum, etc., and makes a charming little pet. Both species of Galago can fold down their large membraneous ears at will. Breeding habits are very similar.

The smaller species is far more good-natured than the larger one, and a family party of four or so, nimbly hopping about the branches of a thorn tree in the moonlight, is a pretty sight.

Their principal natural enemies are the owls (larger), genets and other wild cats, and python. Leopards prey on the larger species.

MISCELLANEOUS OTHER MAMMALS

ROCK HYRAX AND TREE HYRAX

1. ROCK HYRAX

Dendrohyrax brucel hindei (Wroughton)

Field Impression.—A somewhat guineapig-like looking animal, grey brown with no visible tail. An oval, yellow spot in the centre of the back. Usually seen basking, or moving about, on rocky boulders or cliffs, or among the rocks of stony ravines.

Descriptive Notes.—The Hyrax—which is the "Coney" of the Bible—grows as large as a big rabbit. Its closest living relative is the Elephant, to which it is akin in many structural details. The feet all possess hoof-like nails except the inner toe of the hind foot, which is instead furnished with a curved claw. Ears very small and rounded, and muzzle rather bluntly pointed. There is usually a whitish or yellowish spot over each eye, and a more or less yellowish oval spot in the middle of the back. Otherwise it is a general greyish-brown, paler below. With no visible tail, the Rock Hyrax measures up to about 17 inches.

Distribution.—Common in Nairobi National Park. A species of a related Genus, the Large-toothed Hyrax *Procavia capensis mackinderi* (Thomas) is recorded in the Mount Kenya National Park. Common in Tsavo National Park. Common in the Mara and Marsabit National Reserves. So far unrecorded but possibly occurs on the hills at Amboseli.

Habits.—Rock Hyrax should always be watched for when you are passing hills or jumbled boulders on rocky outcrops, or precipitous cliffs or rock faces—in fact similar surroundings to those where one expects to see klipspringers. They are diurnal, but feed mostly at night : spending most of the day basking on the rocks. Their brownish forms are

ROCK HYRAX

CLAW

not easy to distinguish as they sit rather hunched and still, and, except by the observant, they may easily be confused with rounded bits of rock. They are gregarious, and may be seen in large numbers of all ages and sizes : the young ones simply being miniature editions of the parents. Their food is almost entirely vegetable matter.

Their curious, rounded little feet, with rubbery soles, enable them to climb and jump up the steepest rock faces with ease; and when alarmed, they immediately take refuge in rock crevices. They are rather silent animals as a rule, but when alarmed utter high-pitched screeching calls and chattering notes. Their principal enemies are leopards and the larger eagles, and pythons. Rock Hyrax usually deposit their hard, round droppings in regularly resorted-to places, and vast accumulations of such droppings betray their presence. In some cases a thick deposit is formed.

2. THE TREE HYRAX

Dendrohyrax arboreus bettoni (Thomas and Schwann)

Is a closely related species which dwells entirely in trees in more or less thickly forested areas. It is very nocturnal, sleeping in hollows of trees during the day and only coming out to feed after dark, so it is rarely seen. However, at night, it is extremely noisy—uttering piercing, screaming cries which begin with a few cackling notes, and which are immediately answered from all sides. It is about the same size as the Rock Hyrax, but rather greyer in colour with a much finer coat, with usually a whitish spot in the middle of the back. It is usually seen singly, or in pairs. Loring records hearing Tree Hyrax every night in the forst belt of Mount Kenya up to 10,000 feet. He describes the call as beginning with a "series of deep frog-like croaks that gradually gave way to a series of shrill tremulous screams. It was a far-reaching sound and always came from the largest forest trees."

"The dorsal spot (in all Hyrax) consists of a small elongated bare patch, apparently of a glandular nature,

surrounded by a fringe of lighter or darker erectile hairs"
(Shortridge).

The young, of all species, are well-developed at birth,
fully covered with hair, and can run about actively soon
after birth. Three to four in the Rock Hyrax : 1—2 in the
Tree Hyrax. They are born in rock crevices or hollows
of tree respectively.

The Swahili name for the Tree-Hyrax is *Perere*.

ANT-BEAR, OR AARD VARK

Orycteropus afer lademanni (Grote)

(Kiswahili : *Muhanga*)

Field Impression.—A most grotesque, massively built,
short-legged animal, as large as a medium-sized pig, with
long pointed ears, narrow head and rounded snout. Body
sparsely-haired, red-brown. Tail thick at base and tapering
to a point. Very nocturnal.

Descriptive Notes.—The Ant-bear is furnished with
powerful, bear-like claws for digging, which leave a characteristic three-marked track. Its rather rounded, bulky
body slopes gradually into the longish tail rather after the
manner of a Kangaroo. The younger animals are covered
with a thicker coat of bristly reddish-brown or yellowish
hairs, but in adults these become very sparse, imparting
a generally dull earthy hue. The erect, pointed ears, long
narrow head, and pig-like snout are characteristic. Length
of body from 4—4½ feet; tail about 17—24 inches. The
long, narrow viscid tongue which is inserted into antholes
measures (stretched) 18 inches : it can be stretched to at
least double the length of the resting position in the mouth
(Pocock). Weight of an adult may scale up to 140 lb.

Distribution.—Almost everywhere, in all types of country
—though it avoids continuous rocky outcrop. Present in
all the National Parks and National Reserves of Kenya.

Habits.—This extraordinary mammal, which is confined
to Africa, is strictly nocturnal, and very rarely seen by day.

ANT BEAR

It may, therefore, be quite common in an area, and yet never be seen. On the other hand, when driving along the roads or tracks through the veld by night—more especially during the rainy season when the termites on which it preys are most active—the headlights of the car may not infrequently reveal an ant-bear "galumphing" along the track ahead. When alarmed, it moves at a clumsy, bouncing gallop, its long tail stretched out behind and the ears cocked and moving independently of each other like those of a donkey.

The Ant-bear is an intensely powerful creature which can dig at such a rate with its powerful curved claws that it can vanish from sight in a few minutes. The large holes dug by it, in search of white ants, are the principal evidence of its presence in the neighbourhood. These holes are frequently a great nuisance as many a motorist travelling on dirt roads or in the veld has discovered. Numerous animals breed, or lie up, in old ant-bear holes. The burrows are exceedingly deep, generally dug in a sloping direction through the soft earth or sand below the stratum to which the rains penetrate (Powell—Cotton).

Ant-bears feed exclusively on termites and ants, and are exceedingly valuable animals in Africa where termites are such a pest. They dig into the anthills, and then project their long sticky tongues into the passages—so collecting numerous termites at a time.

A single offspring is born in the burrow at a time. Lions, and other large Carnivora, prey upon Ant-bears when they can catch them above ground and more or less in the open.

TEMMINCK'S GROUND PANGOLIN

Manis temmincki (Smuts)

(Kiswahili : *Kakakuona*)

Field Impression.—A quaint, armadillo-like—almost reptile-like mammal, covered with light brown horny scales or plates which overlap one another. It is elongated in form,

GROUND PANGOLIN

with small narrow, earless head and fairly broad, blunt-tipped tail, all covered with overlapping scales. When alarmed, curls up into a ball.

Descriptive Notes.—The body scales are fibrous, considerably indented or serrated, and overlap above and below. Strong curved digging claws furnish the feet; and, like the Ant-bear, the Pangolin has a long, narrow and sticky tongue which it inserts into anthills There is no external ear, and the eyes are small and beady. According to Pitman, there is a soft process, like the end of one's finger, on the under surface of the tail tip which is probably highly sensitive. The tongue, when stretched, extends twelve inches beyond the snout. "The scaly-plating on the back of a mature pangolin is so strong and stream-lined that it will ward off a .303 bullet fired, head on, from a distance of 100 yards" (Adam). As a protective measure, these animals give off a most repulsive odour from certain glands. Length, as a rule, from tip of nose to end of tail, about 3½ feet, but Pitman states that in Uganda it attains as much as 6 feet from nose to tail tip, and is proportionately massive.

Distribution.—These peculiar creatures occur rather uncommonly in all the National Parks and National Reserves of Kenya, though being very strictly nocturnal are but seldom seen.

Habits.—Locally many Europeans describe Pangolins as "Armadillos," but this is wrong, as there are no armadillos in Africa, and they belong to an entirely different group of mammals. The Pangolin—or Scaly Ant-eater—lives almost entirely on termites and ordinary ants : in fact some authorities insist that it appears to prefer ordinary ants to the termites. These it captures by means of its long, viscid tongue, after digging open the nests or anthills with its powerful claws. It has a curious means of locomotion, sometimes moving along almost erect upon its hind limbs, with its body looped over forwards, and holding the short front limbs tucked in; at other times it progresses normally on all fours. When caught in the open it immediately curls up tight into a ball, head tucked beneath broad tail, when it is at once impregnable to ordinary attack. Under these circumstances, if interfered with, it maintains a continuous slapping and grinding motion of the tail against the body, in the hope of catching some convenient part of its adversary between the two. Should this occur, the Pangolin begins to saw backwards and forwards with its tail, and Adam records that he has seen a dog's foreleg almost severed in this manner.

One young is born at a time, and the scales do not harden until the second day. The youngster usually scrambles on to its mother's tail and clings tightly to it, lying across the tail as a rule. The Pangolin occurs in all types of country, including forest and rocky areas. It spends the day in self-created burrows. Closely related species inhabit Asia. Occasionally these quaint creatures may be seen abroad in the very early mornings, or in the glare of car headlights by night.

PORCUPINE

ASPECT WHEN RUNNING
AHEAD OF A CAR AT
NIGHT!

DROPPINGS

PORCUPINE

Hystrix galeata ambigua (Lonnberg)

(Kiswahili : *Nungu*)

Field Impression.—Easily recognisable by its long black and white quills which cover back and tail.

Descriptive Notes.—Total length 2-2½ feet. The quills on the top of the head form a crest of long, thin, wiry bristles, those on the back and tail are stout, lengthy quills— richly banded black and white, with exceedingly sharp points. Lower portion of body clothed with bristly black hairs. The quills of body and tail detach easily, and form suppurating wounds in the feet and jaws of lions and other predators. The feet are equipped with stout digging claws, and the footprint is not unlike that of a small bear. The porcupine is a very powerful rodent. The newly born young have quite soft quills about ¾ inch long.

Distribution.—Common in all the Kenya National Parks and Reserves, but being strictly nocturnal, rarely seen except sometimes by the headlights of a car by night.

Habits.—The presence of porcupines is always indicated by the dropped quills which may be seen from time to time—particularly at the entrance to their burrows. They are fearfully destructive to all root crops, and feed mainly upon roots, bulbs, tubers, the bark of certain trees, and fallen fruits of all kinds. In addition to this they gnaw bones. They issue from their burrows after dark, and as they move about they betray their presence by grunting sounds and the rattle of their quills. When attacked or angered, the porcupine suddenly charges backwards with erect quills vibrating loudly, and a certain number of them will lodge in that part of the adversary which is jabbed by them. Being loosely attached, the quills remain embedded, and even if the greater part is broken off, the tips remain firmly driven in, and unless removed, cause extremely painful, festering sores. Many incautious lions, leopards, or dogs get their paws, or throats, so riddled with porcupine quills that a lingering death from starvation results sooner or later, and I have personally seen a very sick lioness with

CANE RAT

quills visibly projecting from her throat. Many cases of attack on human beings by lions may be attributed to crippling by quills. The popular belief that the Porcupine can "shoot" out its quills is wrong : the short, abrupt but forceful backward rush of the animal jams the quills into its adversary (if he is not wise enough to get out of the way quickly!), and they are automatically detached. Simultaneously, it stamps loudly with one of its back feet.

About 2 young are born as a rule, and the quills appear as a few white soft bristles after about three days. They remain underground until the quills have hardened, when they accompany the mother on her nightly forays. The flesh of the Porcupine makes tender and good eating. Porcupines travel great distances at night in search of especially tempting food—in some cases as much as ten miles. The weght of adults ranges from 40-60 lb. The droppings are characteristic, being formed like very large date stones.

CANE RAT

Thryonomys Sp.
Choerómys Sp.

(Kiswahili : *Ndezi*. Kikuyu : *Ndi*.)

Field Impression.—A very large rodent, shaped rather like a large guineapig, clad in rather spiny, brown hair, and with a fairly short, rat-like tail. Inhabits reedbeds and dense vegetation bordering streams or rivers. When chased into the open it runs like a small pig.

Descriptive Notes.—The rather spiny hairs of the coat (in texture not unlike those of the klipspringer) present a slightly speckled effect, due to the fact that each brown hair has a yellowish band near its tip. Ears short and broadly rounded, muzzle rather broad. The enormous incisor teeth are orange-yellow in colour. There are two genera : a larger one (*Thryonomys*), and a smaller one (*Choeromys*), both similar in appearance and habits, though the smaller one seems to be the common Kenya type. The larger type measures from 12 to 20 inches in body length, with a tail 6-7 inches. Hind foot with four digits; claws strong; tail covered with scales and stiff hairs, twice or more length of hind foot.

Distribution.—Occurs in most swampy areas where there are reedbeds or tall grass, and borders of rivers or streams where the vegetation grows rank.

Habits.—Although called a "rat," this creature is more closely related to the Porcupine. As in the case of the spines of the latter, the Cane Rat's short, flat spiny hairs are loose and detachable in the skin. It dwells among the ranker vegetation where little heaps of closely cut bits of grass stem, together with the oval, fibrous droppings, indicate its presence. It feeds upon various roots, bulbs, grasses and reeds, and is a pest to agricultural grain crops. If alarmed in its haunts at night, it utters a curious booming grunt, and stamps with its hind feet. It is a good swimmer, taking to water readily when pursued. Cane rats can run very fast, dodging nimbly in and out of the herbage. The young are born in shallow depressions lined with grass or shredded reeds in the middle of reedbeds or other rank vegetation. Most carnivora prey greedily upon them, particularly leopards, as well as large hawks and eagles and pythons. The flesh of the Cane Rat makes very good eating, tasting not unlike that of sucking pig!

AFRICAN HARE (UKAMBA CAPE HARE)

Lepus capensis crawshayi (De Winton)

(Kiswahili : *Sungura*)

Field Impression.—Very like a smaller edition of the European Hare, with somewhat similar habits. Seen most often at nights.

Descriptive Notes.—Above mottled sandy-grey, white below. Limbs comparatively long : claws medium, stout, pointed. Ventral surface of tail white. Limbs more or

less suffused with rufous or buff. Back of neck rufous. Length about 18 inches, ears 4-5 inches.

Distribution.—The plains and Savanna country, preferably in fairly open, sandy country.

Habits.—There are two species of Hare in East Africa, of which this is probably the most generally seen in the fairly open country, such as Nairobi National Park, etc. It may very often be disturbed along the roads at night, when its characteristic habit of racing along in front of a car, now and then taking violent leaps to one side or the other (a device to elude pursuit) before finally darting aside into the herbage, is well-known. During the greater part of the day it lies in a "form" under a tussock of grass, or in clumps of bush. The small dry circular droppings may be seen scattered about its feeding area, and it feeds mainly at night. It is a very fast hare, and when disturbed makes off at once at full speed. It may quite often be seen feeding at dusk, or in the very early morning. These hares are preyed on by wild cats of all kinds and leopards and cheetahs, the larger eagles and hawks, large Eagle-owls (*Bubo lacteus*), genets and civets and probably the larger mongooses : and, among snakes, Python and large Mambas. Jackals no doubt account for a few as well.

Two young are the usual number at birth, and these lie close in a "form" under a tuft of grass like those of the European Hare.

Average weight round about 4½ lb.

SQUIRRELS

1. BUSH SQUIRREL

Paraxerus ochraceus jacksoni (De Winton)

(Kiswahili : *Kindi*)

Field Impression. A little greyish-olive squirrel, rather more buffy or yellowish on the limbs, with bushy tail faintly barred with black. Common in the savanna bush country,

BUSH SQUIRREL

GIANT FOREST

SQUIRREL ATTITUDES.

(TANGASSEER RIVER
— NEAR MOIBEN)

and often seen darting across a road, or scolding from a tree. Total length 13-14 inches : tail about 7 inches. Ears small and short and rounded.

Distribution.—Almost everywhere in the lightly bushed or acacia country, and present in all the National Parks and National Reserves of Kenya.

Habits.—This is the common bushveld squirrel of East Africa, and quite frequently seen. It will sit and scold from a tree branch for long intervals, jerking its feathery tail and uttering a noise resembling the whinny of a miniature horse, followed by a long series of "gerzik" notes and chatterings. It lives, and breeds, in the hollows of trees. It is usually observed in pairs, or family parties. Two young are the usual number at a birth. Its principal food consists of wild fruits, berries, seeds and seedpods and other vegetable matter, and probably eggs and nestlings of small birds.

Principal enemies are hawks, owls, wild cats, genets, python, and mamba. The Black Mamba frequently preys on these squirrels.

There are 6 sub-species of *Paraxerus ochraceus* in Kenya.

2. GIANT SQUIRREL

Protoxerus stangeri bea (Heller)

Field Impression.—Larger and more robustly built than the Bush Squirrel : grey, with a reddish tinge above; rusty-red on limbs and underparts, with a white chest. Cheeks rather rusty-coloured, and large bushy tail darker than back, fairly distinctly "ringed" darker.

Distribution.—This, and closely related species, are dwellers in the larger forests, or forest patches, throughout Central and East Africa. The present species is confined to the larger forests of the western districts of Kenya, and I personally saw and sketched examples along the forested margin of the Tangasseer river on the Kapsiliat Estate near Moiben, Eldoret district. It is rather a rare squirrel.

Habits.—These large and very handsome forest squirrels are rather sluggish in their actions. They climb quietly about the branches and limbs of trees, frequently straddling a branch crosswise, with the long graceful tail hanging down—its tip inclining slightly inwards. They can clamber up the broadest and most perpendicular trunks of the large trees, but seem to spend a lot of time searching about for berries, seeds and other food in the undergrowth at the foot of the trees. They appear to be rather silent, and do not chatter and scold like the common Bush Squirrels—at least I did not hear them do so, during the short period in which I was able to observe them.

GROUND SQUIRREL

GROUND SQUIRREL

Euxerus erythropus fulvior (Thomas)

(Kiswahili : *Kidiri*)

Field Impression.—A more robust and bulky looking animal than the Tree and Bush Squirrels. Sandy-rufous, with white underparts, and a conspicuous white stripe along the flanks. Head longer and larger in proportion than that of the Bush Squirrel. Ears very small, rounded, and inconspicuous. Tail flattened and bushy, about 8 inches long. Total length, 16—17 inches.

Distribution.—Ground Squirrels are found almost everywhere in fairly open, more or less sandy country where they dwell in underground warrens in colonies.

Habits.—Ground Squirrels live in warrens, the burrows inter-communicating below the ground, and the burrows are from 4 to 6 feet deep. The squirrels may sometimes be seen scampering along the road, with a peculiar jumping gait, holding their bushy tails level with the ground. Having reached the safety of a burrow, a Ground Squirrel will often stand upright on its hind legs, to gaze at the intruder, before finally popping into the hole. They feed on roots and bulbs, and vegetable matter of many kinds, grain and seeds, also grubs. They are said sometimes to steal poultry eggs and chicks when accessible. Two to six young are born in a burrow, the average being four. There are 2 subspecies in Kenya.

EAST AFRICAN HEDGEHOG

Erinaceus pruneri hindei (Thomas)

(Kiswahili : *Kalunguyeye*)

Field Impression.—The African Hedgehog is rather smaller than the European species, rarely exceeding about 9 inches in length. The back is covered with short, sharp spines :

the forepart of the face is black, and the underparts are white. The young are at first covered with very short, soft spines.

Distribution.—Recorded as common in Nairobi National Park, and at Marsabit, but apparently not recorded from the other National Parks and Reserves, though it probably occurs in most of them. However, it is curiously locally distributed throughout Africa (in various local species) without being common everywhere.

Habits.—The Hedgehog is principally insectivorous, but it also devours worms, slugs, snails, small reptiles, eggs, mice and the young of small ground-nesting birds. It also eats wild fruits and other vegetable matter. It is fond of termites and milk. When alarmed, it curls into a spiny ball. As a general rule, hedgehogs are nocturnal, but occasionally they may be encountered on the move during the day. They make attractive pets, but are usually covered with fleas. From 2—4 young are born. in a nest of dead leaves, and although as many as six have been recorded, four appears to be the usual number. They are preyed upon by a variety of creatures, and are eaten by some native tribes.

JUMPING HARE

SPRING-HARE, OR JUMPING HARE

Pedetes surdaster larvalis (Hollister)

(Kiswahili : *Kamendegere*)

Field Impression.—Another extraordinary African mammal which has the action, and, to a certain extent, the appearance of a kangaroo! Tail long, and rather bushy, and hind legs very long. Ears pointed and eyes very large and dark. Actually all that is usually seen of these nocturnal creatures are their eyes which appear like red globes bobbing along as the hares move in a series of jumps.

Descriptive Notes.—Pale rufous brown above, paler on flanks, and white below. Ears short but rather pointed. Tail, about 1 foot 9 inches in length, bushy at its tip which is black. Hind feet very long, with four toes armed with straight nail-like claws. Front limbs very much shorter, and held close against the chest as the creature proceeds in a series of quick jumps on its hind quarters. Eyes very large, dark brown. Face rather rabbit-like in form. Length of head and body about two feet. There are 3 sub-species of *Pedetes* in Kenya.

Distribution.—Anywhere where the ground is fairly sandy, as it lives in underground burrows in colonies. Exceedingly nocturnal, and seen only near roads by car headlights at night.

Habits.—The usual sight one obtains of a Spring-hare is simply that of a brilliant orange-red globe bouncing along in fascinating manner through the darkness—reflected in the beam of car headlights or a torch! This is caused by the single large eye, as seen in profile, reflecting the light. He moves along with a kangaroo-like, jumping gait. He is often fascinated by the light, and remains to stare at it, thereby presenting an easy mark to the shotgun of the farmer whose crops he has been destroying! As these creatures live in colonies, bobbing lights may be seen all round in such circumstances at night.

Spring-hares live on roots, bulbs, and all manner of green vegetation. A colony consists of four to eight open burrows, each inhabited by a single animal (Heller). The young at birth are extremely large in relation to the size of the adult. Usually one young is produced at a time.

GIANT RAT

Cricetomys gambianus Kenyensis (Osgood)

(Kiswahili : *Buku*)

Field Impression.—A very large, short but coarse haired, rat with a very long, scaly tail—usually with a white tip. Uniform grey-brown, usually with darkish rings round the

GIANT RAT

eyes. Shaped like a common Brown rat but very much larger. Length of head and body 13—15 inches, with tail of 15—17 inches : total length often about 2 feet 3 inches. Face pointed, and ears fairly prominent. Edges of upper lip white. Cheek pouches are present.

Distribution.—Generally a forest dweller, but also frequents thickly wooded thickets, and found in such regions in the Kenya National Parks and Reserves.

Habits.—This large rat is strictly nocturnal and rarely seen by day. I have not seen it in the wild state, but it is said to be timid : not even inclined to bite when caught in a trap. According to Shortridge, it forms burrows of from two to six holes in thickets or dense vegetation, and its holes are often placed at the foot of some forest tree. "It subsists mainly on the seeds of trees, which are said to be stored in holes, and it lives exclusively in dense bush on mountains. A peculiar, wingless cockroach infests it like lice, probably feeding on its stores of food" (Austin Roberts).

In addition to its large size, the white tip to the long tail (though occasionally this feature is lacking), and dark circles round the eyes should aid in close identification.

There are six sub-species in Kenya.

INDEX

Join us and help conserve Wildlife

In the past twenty five years the Society has made a significant contribution of more than $1 000 000 We have exerted an influence through funding research projects; through supplying vehicles, planes and equipment for anti-poaching measures; and through helping education and wildlife awareness.

Every new enrolment will give us more muscle in our negotiations with the Governments, international agencies and organisations who control East Africa's wildlife; and every new subscription will help by increasing our funds, which are used to assist conservation in vital ways.

SWARA makes an ideal present to your relatives and friends—for Christmas, birthdays or special occasions. Please tick the coupon for more forms.

Members gain:

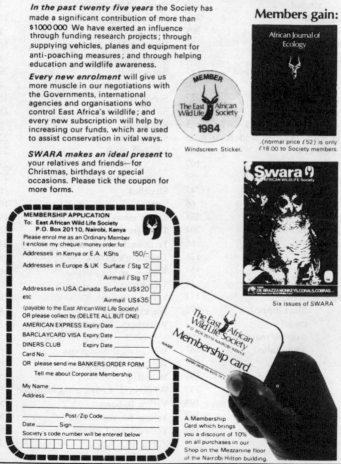

African Journal of Ecology

.(normal price £52) is only £18.00 to Society members.

MEMBER
The East African
Wild Life Society
1984

Windscreen Sticker.

Swara
AFRICAN WILDLIFE Society

DE BRAZZA MONKEYS, CORALS, COBRAS...

Six issues of SWARA

The East African
Wild Life Society
P.O. BOX 20110 NAIROBI KENYA
Membership card
NAME
EXPIRY DATE ON BACK OF C...

A Membership Card which brings you a discount of 10% on all purchases in our Shop on the Mezzanine floor of the Nairobi Hilton building.

232